World War II
The Unseen Visual History

The Caen Memorial

Translated from the French by Christopher Caines

CAEN-NORMANDIE
Mémorial
CITÉ DE L'HISTOIRE POUR LA PAIX

THE NEW PRESS

NEW YORK
LONDON

The New Press gratefully acknowledges the Florence Gould Foundation for supporting the publication of this book.

The original French edition of this book was published to commemorate the inauguration of new exhibition spaces at the Caen Memorial, including the galleries entitled *Guerre mondiale—Guerre totale* (World War—Total War), on May 12, 2010.

Originally published in France as *Guerre mondiale—Guerre totale* by Editions Gallimard/Le Mémorial de Caen, Paris, 2010.
Published in the United States by The New Press, New York, 2011
Distributed by Perseus Distribution

LIBRARY OF CONGRESS CATALOGING-IN-PUBLICATION DATA

Guerre mondiale, guerre totale. English
   World War II : the unseen visual history : the Caen memorial / translated from the French by Christopher Caines.
      p. cm.
   Originally published as : Guerre mondiale—Guerre totale. Paris : Gallimard ; Caen : Mémorial de Caen, c2010.
   "The original French edition of this book was published to commemorate the inauguration of new exhibition spaces at the Caen Memorial, including the galleries entitled Guerre mondiale—Guerre totale (World War—Total War), on May 12, 2010"—T.p. verso.
   Includes bibliographical references.
   ISBN 978-1-59558-681-0 (hc. : alk. paper)   1. World War, 1939–1945—Pictorial works.   I. Caines, Christopher.   II. Mémorial Caen Normandie (Museum)   III. Title.
   D743.2.G8313   2011
   940.53—dc23   2011033968

The New Press was established in 1990 as a not-for-profit alternative to the large, commercial publishing houses currently dominating the book publishing industry. The New Press operates in the public interest rather than for private gain, and is committed to publishing, in innovative ways, works of educational, cultural, and community value that are often deemed insufficiently profitable.

www.thenewpress.com

Composition by dix!
This book was set in Dinot

Printed in the United States of America

10 9 8 7 6 5 4 3 2 1

Acknowledgments

AT THE CAEN MEMORIAL:

Philippe Duron: deputy mayor of Caen; president, Caen Memorial
Stéphane Grimaldi: director, Caen Memorial
Denis Peschanski: professor, CNRS; president, Scientific Advisory Council, Caen Memorial
Pierre Laborie: professor emeritus of contemporary history, University of Toulouse–Le Mirail; member, Scientific Advisory Council, Caen Memorial
Stéphane Simonnet: scientific director, Caen Memorial
Isabelle Bournier: director of cultural affairs, Caen Memorial
Christophe Bouillet: historian, Caen Memorial
Christophe Prime: historian, Caen Memorial
Marie-Claude Berthelot: archivist, Caen Memorial
Jean Quellien: director, Department of History, University of Caen–Basse-Normandie; member, Scientific Advisory Council, Caen Memorial
Gérard Rabinovitch: philosopher, sociologist; researcher, CNRS Centre de Recherches: Sens, Éthique, Société (CERSES)

Cartography by Guillaume Balavoine, adapted by Édigraphie

AT ÉDITIONS GALLIMARD:

Editorial director: Élisabeth de Farcy
Design director: Alain Gouessant
Editor: Olivia Barbet-Massin
Design and book dummy: Virginie Lafon, Frédéric Savarit
Copy editors: Emmanuel de Saint-Martin, Marie-Paule Rochelois
Production: Amélie Airiau, under the direction of Christian Delval
Project liaison to the Caen Memorial: Madeleine Giai-Levra
Press and communications: Valérie Tolstoï, David Ducreux

Contents

World War—Total War
by Pierre Laborie

Preface: The Twentieth Century Was Ten Years Old

A hundred years ago, people the world over lived in a state of carefree self-delusion, a complacent faith in social and industrial progress, medical advances, the system of colonial empires—not to mention the wonder of electricity and gas on every floor or the great universal expositions.

Four years later, World War I, ignited by a spark, would plunge Europe and indeed the entire world into total chaos in a way no one could foresee or even conceive. Only Jean Jaurès—the socialist politician and committed pacifist who worked tirelessly to prevent the outbreak of hostilities between France and Germany—predicted the worst.

Everything followed on from there: two world wars, the horrors of totalitarianism, the bankruptcy of humanism at Treblinka and Auschwitz, tens of millions killed—civilians and soldiers, children and adults—and then at last, like the exit from a nightmare, a promise of rebuilding the international moral order: the Universal Declaration of Human Rights, promulgated on December 10, 1948. This act of faith that united forty-three states has since its signing nonetheless prevented neither war, nor injustice, nor even further genocides.

Our own new century is now ten years old. Already, it seems fragile. The events of September 11, 2001, seem to have set its tone in a decade marked by new forms of religious and political obscurantism and by violent acts of revenge against colonialism. It is a decade marked equally by an ecological devastation that is well under way and which, if humanity persists in its willful blindness, will result in still further irreversible threats.

The twentieth century, although it began laden with dreams and ideals, witnessed a great human disaster whose innumerable sufferings no memorial could ever contain. Nonetheless, the idea of a truly moral system of global governance always seems to be breaking down, and to remain always remote from political and economic realities. The selfishness of the rich countries always seems to trump their judgment and understanding, while fanaticisms of every kind thrive, as always, on the misery of one part of humanity, which the indecent comfort of the other part renders ever more unacceptable.

This is why the Caen Memorial exists.

To be sure, the museum's influence is modest, but it emerged from a concerted attempt to make sense of and to provide a perspective on history and the teaching of history, and to assert the rightful place of history in the space of public debate. We believe, in effect, that a society without history, a society that fails to accept this essential, fundamental construction of memory and to comprehend its collective dimension, is doomed to gradually lose its bearings.

Every year some 400,000 people visit the Caen Memorial, including 120,000 primary, middle, and secondary school students, prepared in advance and accompanied by their teachers. It is they who will be the leading teachers of the next generation.

Essentially the Memorial itself and this book constitute, in a sense, acts of faith in the idea that our societies need history, thirst for it—for the teaching of the social and cultural aspects of history at every level, from the universal to the simply familial.

Our museum is now undergoing the most extensive transformation since its founding, one of the results of which is this book. With the generous help of numerous historians, including Denis Peschanski and Pierre Laborie, we have sought to revive in this museum the extraordinary audacity initially imagined by its founder, a true humanist and great European, Jean-Marie Girault. As a young law student, Girault went to the aid of the civilian victims of the bombing of Caen. He knew at first hand the horrors of war.

This is why the Memorial in Caen, a city scarred by history and devoted to peace, has such a vital place in evolving European society—above all as a focus for reflection and dialogue between memory and history, between expert and novice, between student and teacher, between parents and children.

If you enjoy this book, the fruit of many years' work by a team of passionately devoted collaborators, come visit us in Caen. ■

PHILIPPE DURON,
Deputy Mayor of Caen
President, Caen Memorial

STÉPHANE GRIMALDI,
Director, Caen Memorial

ISABELLE BOURNIER,
Director of Cultural Affairs
Caen Memorial

Foreword: Memory as the Object of History

By the mid-1980s, Jean-Marie Girault, then the mayor of Caen, had decided to build a great memorial: a war museum devoted to the cause of peace. It soon became clear to him that the Normandy Campaign could only be understood in the context of World War II as a whole. By the same token, he realized that any attempt to understand the Invasion of Normandy—which is too often reduced only to the epic story of D-Day itself, extraordinary though that battle was—and the general collapse into war and death and the heroic struggle that constituted the conflict as a whole, leads necessarily to more general reflections on war and peace.

From the outset, Girault made the gamble—daring at the time—of bringing in a group of scholars known as the "new French historians," who gravitated around the Institut d'Histoire du Temps Présent (IHTP; the Institute of Contemporary History), a branch of the Centre National de la Recherche Scientifique (CNRS; the National Center for Scientific Research, a federally funded research institute). As a young member of this group who worked on the project in its early stages, I remember what an extraordinary adventure it was—until shortly after the Memorial opened on June 6, 1988, when other, less scientific approaches were adopted that led to a retreat from Girault's initial bold gamble in linking the most highly specialized, cutting-edge research with the most outstanding museum design.

Because our understanding of the period covered by the Memorial has deepened while its initial museological approach has become outdated, and because in general the time had come to reaffirm the respect for our visitorship that must always remain the Memorial's hallmark, Stéphane Grimaldi decided, upon accepting the post of director of the Memorial in 2007, to revive and reinvigorate the museum's scientific advisory board, which brings together historians, museum specialists, and educators. Together, Grimaldi and his team embarked upon a genuine renovation of the Memorial, including the inauguration of new exhibition spaces that feature displays devoted to the phenomena of world war and total war.

Each visitor will be able to judge for him or herself the validity of the new museological approach. Like the museum's original, chronologically organized galleries, the new sequence of displays reflects the conviction that the exhibitions themselves must guide the visitor through a coherent tour. Rather than leaving him to wander, we take the visitor by the hand. There is no one truth in history, and each visitor, to be sure, will form her own ideas. Yet it is a real *reading* that the

>>>

>>> Memorial proposes, of a "book" composed of images and texts discovered page by page—relying, of course, upon the most up-to-date museological techniques.

By bringing in Pierre Laborie, former professer at the University of Toulouse–Le Mirail and later a professor at the École des Hautes Études en Sciences Sociales in Paris (EHESS; the School of Advanced Studies in Social Sciences)—and the historian who revolutionized the study of French public opinion during the *années noires* (the "dark years" of Nazi occupation)—we knew we could rely on a researcher who not only enjoys an international reputation but also has always been interested in the two key questions for this kind of museum: How do we articulate memory and history? And how do we incorporate within a museum, and thus share with a very wide public, the most recent advances in knowledge? You will judge our success for yourself by virtue of this book and when you make your next visit to the Memorial, but I am convinced that the gamble has paid off.

I would like to note four further points. First, the museum's increased attention to the extermination of the Jews of Europe. Until recently the Memorial failed to accord the Shoah its rightful place and the significance that it deserves in the main galleries. We have emphasized two analytical perspectives. An examination of what Pierre Laborie has rightly termed the *extermination de proximité* (extermination at close range) enables us to emphasize the major change in historical paradigm resulting from awareness that the extermination in the East took a wholly different form than it did in the West. Although the "Shoah by bullets" remains relatively little known, that is not because it was carried out in secrecy, for the massacres took place in full view and with the full knowledge of local communities mobilized for the purpose; moreover, the modus operandi involved neither gas chambers nor death camps. Such absolute savagery was already well known to the inhabitants of the former Soviet Union and, in recent years, the period has become the subject of preliminary historical research. Above all, the work of Father Patrick Desbois (author of *The Holocaust by Bullets: A Priest's Journey to Uncover the Truth Behind the Murder of 1.5 Million Jews*, which concerns the *Einsatzgruppen*, the SS paramilitary death squads, in Ukraine), with his systematic campaign to locate the mass graves in the former USSR and to gather eyewitness accounts, has made it possible to reveal both the singular character and the vast scale of the atrocities. We could never thank him enough for choosing the Memorial as a place to display the results of his efforts in a permanent exhibition. However, without denying the uniqueness of the extermination of the Jews, the Memorial situates it within a period of mass violence of an extreme level of brutality that included the murder of the mentally ill in Nazi Germany and the deaths of millions of Soviet prisoners of war and also, before the war, the massacres of Chinese citizens of Nanjing by the Japanese.

Second, and in the same spirit, the renovated museum has expanded its coverage to address the full geopolitical scope of the combat. The Pacific War was already covered in the Memorial, but it is now explored more thoroughly in the context of total global war. To an even greater degree, perhaps, the Eastern Front is at last given due consideration. For obvious political and ideological reasons, the role of the Soviet forces had been steadily undervalued since the war, year after year. It seemed that the Cold War and the subsequent collapse of the Soviet Union somehow justified our putting behind us this decisive aspect of our history—to such an extent that we must now insist on recalling that the liberation of France itself was due as much to the Red Army, which confronted the bulk of the German and Axis forces, as to the Allied troops who landed in Normandy on that day in June 1944.

In the context of wartime, it is always difficult to give daily life its rightful place in history. At the Memorial, the experiences of both military personnel and of civilians behind the front lines are extensively documented so that the visitor may assess what world war and total war meant for entire communities.

Objects, films, and documents of all kinds are provided to account for the complexity of aspects of the war too long distorted by the tendency to view them in black-and-white terms—including, most importantly, responses to the Allied aerial bombardment of cities and civilian populations, which has been obscured for far too long. The people of Caen—a city almost entirely obliterated by Allied bombing in the three months following D-Day—indeed know something about this.

I would like to close with the question posed by the museum's final displays, which depart from the chronological and thematic presentation that predominates up to that point. Before recalling the Battle of Normandy one last time, we pose the crucial question of memory: What have we done with this history of blood and tears? The point is not to oppose the scientific approach of the historian to the inevitable flaws of individual or collective memory. This reductive opposition has had its day. What we propose rather is the historian's analysis of the phenomenon of memory itself: that is, memory as an *object* of historical study. This issue sums up in a way the ambition of the whole new sequence of galleries even as it governs the renovation of the entire museum now underway: how to confront the dual challenge of incorporating the most recent advances in knowledge and making them accessible to a broad public. ▪

DENIS PESCHANSKI
Senior Researcher, CNRS
President of the Scientific Advisory Council,
Caen Memorial

The Failure of Peace

NOVEMBER 1918–AUGUST 1939

Parade of war-wounded and amputees on the Champs-Élysées in honor of Armistice Day, November 11, 1918.
© Rue des Archives

The Legacy of the Great War

Because of its violence—the matrix out of which the entire twentieth century will emerge—World War I is a catastrophe without precedent. With 10 million dead and 21 million wounded, most of them military personnel, the conflict is an immense bloodletting from which Europe emerges traumatized. An entire generation of men disappears into the trenches, leaving behind millions of widows and orphans. The burden of so many dead weighs heavily on the living. Collective mourning and wounds both physical and psychological undermine the values of a continent in ruins, a Europe that no longer rules the world. Victors and vanquished alike emerge broken from the trial by fire. "Civilizations are mortal," writes the poet Paul Valéry, encapsulating the widespread disarray left in the wake of a war that was supposed to be the last. But the dream of a "war to end all wars" is forced to confront the crises, stresses, and revolutionary movements of a new world order even more unstable than the one washed away in 1914. ●

French soldiers in a frontline trench, Verdun, 1916.
© Rue des Archives

The ossuary and cemetery of Douaumont, in Meuse, northeastern France.
© Roger Viollet

NOVEMBER 9, 1918
COLLAPSE OF THE GERMAN EMPIRE.

MARCH 4, 1919
MOSCOW: LENIN FOUNDS THE COMMUNIST INTERNATIONAL.

JANUARY 10, 1920
THE CHARTER OF THE LEAGUE OF NATIONS GOES INTO EFFECT.

F M A M J J A S O N D J F M A M J J A S O N D J F M A M J J A S O N D J F M A M
1919   1920   1921

NOVEMBER 11, 1918
THE ARMISTICE BETWEEN GERMANY AND THE ALLIES ENDS WORLD WAR I.

JUNE 28, 1919
SIGNING OF THE TREATY OF VERSAILLES WITH GERMANY.

MARCH 12, 1921
THE TREATY OF RIGA SETS THE BORDER BETWEEN EUROPE AND SOVIET RUSSIA.

President Wilson signs the Treaty of Versailles on June 28, 1919, in the Hall of Mirrors at Versailles. This photo appeared in *L'Illustration* on July 12, two weeks later.
© L'Illustration

After the disaster of the Great War, avant-garde artists express the vital need Europeans feel to transgress conservative social values. With the arrival of American jazz and the birth of Dadaism, the Roaring Twenties begin— an era that will witness a profound questioning of traditional values across the continent.

FROM RIGHT TO LEFT: composer Georges Auric, painter Francis Picabia, writer Georges Ribemont-Dessaignes, Picabia's wife Germaine Everling, composer Alfredo Casella, and writer/performer Tristan Tzara (with Dada written on his forehead), 1921.
© Bibliothèque Jacques Doucet, Paris

The Failure of the "Victors' Peace"

Peace treaties among the victorious powers and each of the defeated countries put an end to the Great War. The European continent is utterly transformed by the disappearance of the German, Austro-Hungarian, Russian, and Ottoman empires, leaving behind small, fragile nationalist states. The most important of the treaties is concluded with Germany. In the Hall of Mirrors at the Palace of Versailles—the very place where the German Empire had been founded in 1871—the young Weimar Republic is forced to sign a humiliating accord, a peace without concessions from the victors, a treaty that German public opinion considers a *Diktat*. Even though the Paris Peace Conference also sees the founding of the League of Nations, a permanent international organization designed in theory to broker peaceful solutions to conflicts between states, peace is weakened and democracy threatened across Europe. ●

APRIL 16, 1922
THE TREATY OF RAPALLO SIGNED BY GERMANY AND THE USSR.

A S O N D J F M A M J J A S O N D J F M A M J J A S O N D J F M A M J J A S O N
1922   1923   1924

OCTOBER 29, 1922
FASCIST LEADER MUSSOLINI TAKES POWER IN ITALY.

Fascist leader
Benito Mussolini.
© Rue des Archives

Hitler exits the hall after giving a
speech at a meeting of the NSDAP,
the Nazi Party.
© DITE

The Rise of Totalitarianism

Accorded an exceptional degree of prestige and trust
after the war, the liberal democracies soon reveal
how fragile they really are. The giddy atmosphere in
artistic circles and the unbuttoned social mores of the
Roaring Twenties conceal as much as they express the
profound crisis of societies confronted by runaway infla-
tion, punishing national debt, and ideologies opposed to
democratic principles. Given the economic difficulties, the
humiliations entailed by the peace treaties, and the fear of
Communist revolution, authoritarian regimes find fertile
soil across Europe. Benito Mussolini's fascist movement
takes power in Italy in 1922. In Germany, political un-
rest, the Bolshevik-inpired Sparticist movement, and
the abortive coup d'état attempted by Adolf Hitler and
the Nazi Party in Munich in 1923 (the Beer Hall Putsch)
all undermine the Weimar Republic. Most of the countries of Western Europe and Southern Europe fall into the
hands of dictators. The Great Depression that begins in
1929 strikes not only the world's brand-new economic
superpower, the U.S., but engulfs Europe in dire poverty
and mass unemployment. The crisis exacerbates social
tensions, weakens political institutions, and favors the
rise of the far right. ●

A bank note worth 500 million
marks, 1923.
Caen Memorial

OCTOBER 15–16, 1925
THE TREATY OF LOCARNO RATIFIES THE STATUS QUO OF GERMANY'S WESTERN
BORDERS WITH FRANCE AND BELGIUM AGREED TO IN THE TREATY OF VERSAILLES.

AUGUST 27, 1928
THE KELLOGG–BRIAND
PACT PROHIBITS WAR.

M A M J J A S O N D J F M A M J J A S O N D J F M A M J J A S O M D J F M A M J J A S O N

1926   **1927**   **1928**

1927
STALIN TAKES SOLE POWER
AS DICTATOR OF THE USSR.

Nazi Germany

In a country ravaged by crisis, Adolf Hitler, having taken power legally as chancellor of the Reich in January 1933, transforms Germany into a totalitarian state. Starting in 1933, the first concentration camps are opened to imprison and punish opponents of the regime. The Nazi Party becomes a mass organization that recruits and controls the entire society, mobilizing Germans by means of colossal, meticulously staged gatherings such as the annual Nazi Party congresses held in Nuremberg from 1933 to 1938 (the Nuremberg Rallies). Nazi Germany, which intends to create a "new man," submits to a political hierarchy with Hitler as its *Führer*, its leader and guide. Established as the regime's official ideology, racism and anti-Semitism are enforced by an array of administrative measures and laws excluding Jews from public life and the national community. German exiles try to warn the world of the Nazi threat but are ignored by democratic governments that fail to grasp the true nature of the Nazi regime. ●

Hitler addresses the Nazi Party at the Nuremberg Rally, 1938. Photograph by Roger Schall for *Paris-Match*. © Roger Schall

The annual Nazi Party Congress in Nuremberg in 1938 takes place against the backdrop of a gigantic grandstand and a colonnade topped by towering beams piercing the night sky, the so-called "cathedral of light." © Roger Schall

JULY 13, 1931
BANKING CRISIS IN AUSTRIA AND GERMANY; FOREIGN INVESTORS HASTILY WITHDRAW THEIR CAPITAL.

JANUARY 30, 1933
HITLER TAKES POWER AS CHANCELLOR IN BERLIN.

M A M J J A S O N D J F M A M J J A S O N D J F M A M J J A S O N D J F M A M J J A S O N

1930   **1931**   **1932**

OCTOBER 24, 1929
BLACK TUESDAY: THE NEW YORK STOCK MARKET CRASHES.

SEPTEMBER 18–19, 1931
JAPANESE FORCES INVADE MANCHURIA.

Entry of German troops into the Rhineland, March 8, 1936.
© Roger Viollet

The Road to War

Eager to erase the results of the Treaty of Versailles and to acquire *Lebensraum* (living space—land and natural resources) for the "Aryan" people and the new Germany, Adolf Hitler violates international law in a series of military strikes: he rearms Germany, remilitarizes the Rhineland, and annexes Austria with the *Anschluss*. Next, Hitler is allowed to annex the Sudetenland from Czechoslovakia at the Munich Conference on Security Policy in September 1938; he engages in a rapprochement with fascist Italy and the military regime of Japan; and he does not hestitate, in a sort of alliance of dictators, to intervene militarily in the Spanish Civil War on the side of Franco's fascists. Still traumatized by the slaughter of World War I, longing to avoid a new war at all costs, and eager to view Hitler as a bulwark against Bolshevism, France and Great Britain remain passive in the face of the rising tide of the fascist dictatorships' threats and aggression. On August 23, 1939, Germany and the USSR sign a nonaggression pact. The news stuns the governments of the democracies, for the two countries seem to be irreconcilable ideological adversaries. War now becomes unavoidable. On September 1, 1939, Germany invades Poland. Two days later, Great Britain and France declare war on the Third Reich. ●

The people of Austria welcome Hitler as he enters Vienna, March 14, 1938.
© Roger Viollet

The front page of the daily *Le Journal* for October 2, 1938; the lead stories analyze the consequences of the Munich Accord.
Caen Memorial

OCTOBER 3, 1935
THE ITALIAN ARMY INVADES ABYSSINIA.

JULY
MILIT
THE S
SPAN

F M A M J J A S O N D J F M A M J J A S O N D J F M A M J J A S O N D J F M A
1934   1935   1936

MARCH 24, 1933
THE ENABLING ACT GIVES HITLER DICTATORIAL POWERS FOR FOUR YEARS.

NIGHT OF JUNE 29–30, 1934
THE NIGHT OF THE LONG KNIVES: HITLER'S "BLOOD PURGE" OF THE RANKS OF THE NAZI PARTY'S PARAMILITARY WING, THE STURMABTEILUNG, OR SA, WHICH HAD PLAYED A KEY ROLE IN HIS RISE TO POWER; OTHER CRITICS OF THE NAZIS ARE ALSO ATTACKED, JAILED, OR KILLED. AFTER THE PURGE, THE SA IS SUPERSEDED BY THE SS.

MARCH 7
HITLER
THE RH

The German–Soviet Nonaggression Pact

The Munich Accord of 1938 in no way hinders Hitler's aggressive policy of territorial conquest, which reaches a new level in early 1939 when he demands the Danzig Corridor, a narrow strip of Polish territory (formerly part of West Prussia) that would connect Germany to the Free City of Danzig, with its vital harbor on the Baltic Sea. When Warsaw, pressured by Paris and London, refuses, Hitler prepares for war against Poland. To ensure victory, he does not hesitate to make peace with his worst enemy, the USSR, which has kept itself apart from the European game of alliances, and which the Western democracies actively seek to rally to their cause to protect Poland. Aware of the danger posed by having to wage war on two fronts, Hitler catches the Allies off-guard by signing a nonaggression pact with the Soviets on August 23, 1939, in Moscow. That signature explodes like a bomb across Europe. A secret protocol anticipates an eventual partition of Poland between the two powers and the establishment of separate spheres of influence in the Baltics. From now on, the German Chancellor is free to make war in Western Europe. ●

Stalin and the German foreign minister, Joachim von Ribbentrop, seal the Molotov–Ribbentrop pact (officially, the Treaty of Nonaggression between Germany and the USSR) with a handshake on August 23, 1939. German photos of the event were retouched by the Nazi propaganda ministry. LEFT: A retouched image on the cover of the *Berliner Illustrierte Zeitung*; RIGHT: an unretouched photo on the cover of the French magazine *L'Illustration*.
© Service Historique de la Défense

The front page of the daily *Paris-Soir*, August 23, 1939, announcing the German–Soviet pact.
Caen Memorial

...NY AGAINST ...EPUBLIC: THE ...WAR BEGINS.

JULY 7, 1937
THE SINO-JAPANESE WAR BEGINS.

SEPTEMBER 29–30, 1938
THE MUNICH CONFERENCE: FRANCE AND GREAT BRITAIN ACCEDE TO THE DISMEMBERMENT OF CZECHOSLOVAKIA.

AUGUST 23, 1939
A NONAGRESSION PACT IS SIGNED BY GERMAN FOREIGN MINISTER RIBBENTROP AND SOVIET FOREIGN MINISTER MOLOTOV IN STALIN'S PRESENCE.

S O N D J F M A M J J A S O N D J F M A M J J A S O N D J F M A M J J A S O N
1937   1938   1939

...IZES

NOVEMBER 1, 1936
PROCLAMATION OF THE ROME–BERLIN AXIS.

MARCH 12, 1938
THE ANSCHLUSS: AUSTRIA JOINS THE THIRD REICH.

MARCH 15, 1939
THE CZECH LANDS OF BOHEMIA AND MORAVIA ARE OCCUPIED BY GERMAN FORCES.

German tanks on the move during the Battle of France, May–June 1940.
© BAVCC

The Dark Years: France Under Nazi Occupation

The Onslaught

Germany's invasions, first of Poland, starting on September 1, 1939, then of France, starting on May 10, 1940, stun and paralyze the conquered countries. France's trauma is well expressed by the title of soldier-historian Marc Bloch's 1940 book analyzing the causes of the disaster, *Strange Defeat*. Overwhelmed by the speed and scale of their loss, the French public puts its trust in World War I hero Marshal Pétain, allowing him to launch an authoritarian "National Revolution" and a repressive campaign of "moral and intellectual renewal." In a period of onerous restrictions, constant shortages, economic plunder, and conscripted labor, Pétain's Vichy government, which openly chooses to collaborate with the occupying forces, hunts down the ever more numerous members of the Resistance, and hands over both French Jews and Jewish refugees to the Nazis, plunging France inexorably into one of the darkest periods in its history, the "dark years." ●

NEAR RIGHT: **Soldiers gather** for a few moments of relaxation.
© ECPAD

FAR RIGHT: **Fearing that Paris would be bombed** after September 1, 1939, the authorities posted evacuation routes to enable drivers to escape the capital as quickly as possible.

German soldiers breach the German–Polish frontier, September 1, 1939.
© Rue des Archives

The Phony War

Two days after the invasion of Poland, France reluctantly declares war on Germany. Confident in their inevitable victory and the invincibility of their army, the generals deploy their forces along the heavily fortified Maginot Line (France's entire eastern border with Germany and Belgium), preparing for another "war of position," the dug-in trench warfare of World War I. As if by tacit agreement between the opposing armies, the soldiers find themselves engaged in a "phony war" (a term coined by journalist Roland Dorgèles)—a truce characterized by eight long months of agonized waiting for real battle to begin, punctuated by occasional rest leaves. The tedium is relieved only by various pastimes, variety shows, and rallies organized as much to reassure public opinion as to maintain the troops' morale. ●

Civil defense posters, from a series designed to inform people about such issues as (top to bottom) bombs, gas attack, and bomb shelters. Original size: 31 x 24 in. (80 x 60 cm).
Caen Memorial

France's 5 million troops included 1 million workers on "special assignment" who retained their civilian jobs while under military jurisdiction. Many worked in mines or factories; some, like those pictured behind the soldiers in this photo, dug and built earthworks at the front.
© ECPAD

German troops parade along the Champs-Élysées in Paris, June 14, 1940.
© Roger Schall

The Battle of France

Hitler launches his *Blitzkrieg* (lightning war) on May 10, 1940, with simultaneous aerial bombardment and attack by armored divisions against the Netherlands, Belgium, Luxembourg, and France. Four days later, the Wehrmacht outflanks the Maginot Line, crossing through Belgium and the Ardennes forest and driving deep into French territory as far as the city of Sedan. On May 17, Paul Reynaud, the newly elected prime minister, appeals to Marshal Pétain, the hero of the Battle of Verdun in World War I, appointing him minister of state the next day. The blinding speed of the German army's advance toward Paris—the French lines are breached at the Somme on June 6, 1940, only some 70 miles from the capital—drives thousands of people to flee their homes. Unnerved by the threat, the French government abandons Paris for Tours on June 10, then moves to Bordeaux on June 14. The total collapse of the French army on every front leaves the nation with a deep and lasting trauma. After barely five weeks of fighting, 92,000 French soldiers and 28,000 civilians are dead, with 250,000 wounded and missing in action, and 1.65 million taken prisoners of war. Pétain, who succeeds Raynaud as the last prime minister of the Third Republic on June 16, immediately makes overtures for an armistice with Germany. ●

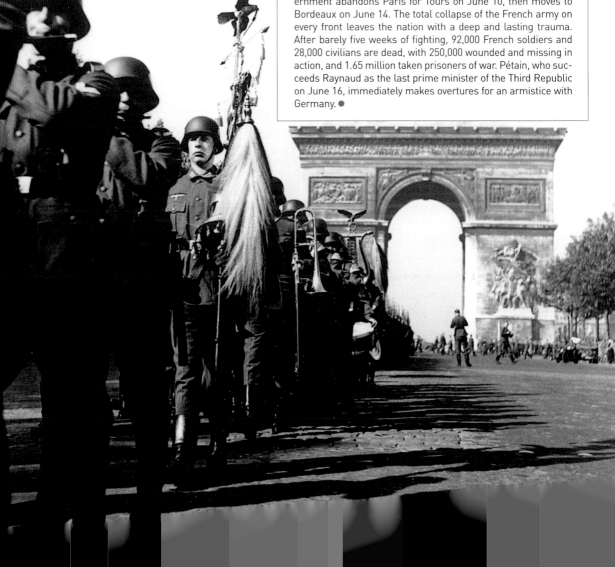

A TOUS LES FRANÇAIS

La France a perdu une bataille!
Mais la France n'a pas perdu la guerre!

Des gouvernants de rencontre ont pu capituler, cédant à la panique, oubliant l'honneur, livrant le pays à la servitude. Cependant, rien n'est perdu!

Rien n'est perdu, parce que cette guerre est une guerre mondiale. Dans l'univers libre, des forces immenses n'ont pas encore donné. Un jour, ces forces écraseront l'ennemi. Il faut que la France, ce jour-là, soit présente à la victoire. Alors, elle retrouvera sa liberté et sa grandeur. Tel est mon but, mon seul but!

Voilà pourquoi je convie tous les Français, où qu'ils se trouvent, à s'unir à moi dans l'action, dans le sacrifice et dans l'espérance.

Notre patrie est en péril de mort.
Luttons tous pour la sauver!

VIVE LA FRANCE !

18 JUIN 1940

GÉNÉRAL DE GAULLE

A poster issued shortly after General Charles de Gaulle's Appeal of June 18, broadcast from London by the BBC. "France has lost a battle!" it reads. "But France has not lost the war!"
Caen Memorial

Hitler on the esplanade of the Trocadéro, Paris, June 23, 1940.
© Gamma

Germany's General Keitel hands the text of the 1940 armistice to France's General Huntziger, June 22, 1940.
© Bundesarchiv

The Armistice

A fervent defender of making peace with Germany, Pétain addresses the French people over the radio for the first time on June 17, 1940 to announce talks between the two nations. The next day, over the BBC network, Charles de Gaulle, who served briefly as undersecretary of state for national defense and war in the Reynaud cabinet, and has recently been promoted to the rank of brigadier general (though this has not been publicly announced), rejects any idea of armistice or defeat, and urges the French to resist and continue the fight. However, by this point, the French defeat is virtually a fait accompli. In a clearing in the forest of Compiègnes, near the tiny village of Rethondes, in the very same train car in which Germany had surrendered and signed the Armistice of November 11, 1918, Hitler convenes the French representatives to announce to them the conditions of the new armistice. Signed on June 22 by General Huntziger, chairman of the French delegation, and General Keitel, chief of the Supreme Command of the Armed Forces and effectively the Nazi war minister, the armistice disarms the French fleet, reduces the army to 100,000 men, and splits the country into several zones, the largest of which are the Zone of Occupation in the north under German military rule and the so-called Free Zone controlled by the Vichy regime in the south. ●

A London double-decker bus protrudes from a gaping pit left by German bombing during the Blitz, which lasted from September 1940 to May 1941.
© Rue des Archives

A cartoon by David Low for the *Evening Standard* on September 24, 1940: "Gad, Sir John, Beaverbrook is right. We must show Hitler we have command of the air, the seas, the land and the Underground."
© DR

The Battle of Britain

Deprived of its French ally, Great Britain now confronts Germany alone, and finds itself in turn threatened with invasion. United behind Prime Minister Winston Churchill, the British are determined to resist. After the British rejection of his peace proposal in July 1940, Hitler unleashes the Luftwaffe over the country in pursuit of three objectives: to eliminate Britain's fighter squadrons, destroy its military and industrial infrastructure, and deny British convoys access to the English Channel. After the initial phase of the air war (August 13–23), in which British fighters prevail against German bombers, German raids reach their maximum intensity from late August to early September. On the eve of the London Blitz (September 7–30), the British fighters are exhausted. But beginning on September 7, in response to the Royal Air Force's bombing of Berlin on August 26, Hitler abandons his campaign against RAF fighter airfields—inadvertently saving the fighter squadrons from total destruction—in order to concentrate on the bombing of London and its suburbs. Almost 7,000 Londoners are killed by German incendiary bombs in September, and 15,000 more are injured or killed the following month. But confronted with heroic British resistance and heavy German losses, and deprived of the aerial supremacy required by his plan for invasion, Hitler is forced to postpone planned German landings in spring 1941.

During the 80 days of the Battle of Britain, the Germans lose 2,300 planes—their first setback since the beginning of the war. But the British victory is purchased at great cost by the unshakeable courage of the British people and the pilots of the RAF. ●

A cartoon by David Low for the *Evening Standard* of June 18, 1940: "Very well, alone."
© DR

Marshal Pétain, the Vichy head of state, meets Hitler for the first time, at the little train station of Montoire-sur-le-Loir, on October 24, 1940, signifying the start of official French collaboration with the Nazis.
Caen Memorial

Collaboration

The military debacle and defeat of 1940 are so traumatic for most of the French that some turn to Marshal Pétain as a father figure, investing in him their hopes for national salvation. On July 10, 1940, the French Chamber of Deputies transfers all its powers to Pétain, dissolving the Third Republic, democracy, parliament, and itself. Pétain replaces the traditional revolutionary ideals of "Liberty, Equality, Fraternity" with a new slogan: "Work, Family, Fatherland." Pétain and his government advance a new political program called National Revolution: a return to the "true" values of order, discipline, family, corporatism, small farming, cottage industry, etc. The new authoritarian regime rapidly adopts the tactics of the ruling European fascist regimes: a repressive police state dominated by the Milice (a new paramilitary organization that collaborates with the Germans against the Resistance), persecution of the regime's opponents, individual and mass arrests, and ultimately openly declared collaboration with the occupying Nazis. Pétain loyalists Jacques Doriot, Pierre Laval, and Admiral François Darlan soon become the principal figures in the policy of collaboration, which begins officially on October 24, 1940 in a ceremony in Montoire. In 1941 Darlan is named Commander of the French Armed Forces and Pétain's deputy; in 1942 he becomes minister for the interior, defense, and foreign affairs, and de facto head of the Vichy government. ●

Pierre Laval, who served two terms as prime minister in the Vichy government, attends the ceremony in Compiègne marking the arrival of the first train bearing French prisoners of war repatriated in the program known as the Relève (Relief), in 1942. Each prisoner was exchanged for one French worker who went to labor in Germany industry.
© Roger Viollet

Jacques Doriot, founder of the ultra-nationalist Parti Populaire Français (PPF) and a figurehead of the Vichy regime's policy of collaboration. Doriot co-founded the Légion des Volontaires Français (LVF), a French unit of the Wehrmacht, and later joined the Wehrmacht itself.
© La Documentation Française

French Officers in the Concentration Camps of the Third Reich

After the French defeat of June 1940, between 25,000 and 30,000 French officers vanish into the closed world of the Nazi Oflag (*Offizierslager,* or Officers' Camps) POW system. These camps are built hastily, usually within existing military encampments, all over the territory occupied by the Reich, including Poland, Austria, and Czechoslovakia. In accordance with the Geneva Conventions, the imprisoned officers are exempt from any labor. Crowded into small spaces, condemned to indeterminate detention, waiting for mail and parcels from home, they struggle to overcome the ordeal of captivity while resisting Nazi and Vichy propaganda. Many attempt to escape, but many fail. Through their encounters in the camps with exceptional men in every cultural and intellectual field, the officers confront their demoralizing idleness by improvising courses of study and self-improvement, and envisioning France after the war. ●

Fol's Sag's, a theater troupe formed by prisoners of Stalag VIIIC, in Sagan, Silesia, near the city of Breslau (modern Wrocław, Poland), performed plays and reviews with elaborate sets and costumes and a live orchestra.
Caen Memorial

Prisoners play soccer on the athletic fields of Stalag VIIIC, October 1943.
Caen Memorial

The so-called smiling firing-squad victim, the imperturbable Resistance fighter Georges Blind, defies his fate. Blind survives this mock execution, intended to make him talk. Later deported, he will die in Upper Silesia in an Auschwitz satellite camp in late 1944.
© FNDIRP

Resistance

Shortly after the shock of the French defeat and the occupation of the northern half of France by German forces, the Resistance begins to form: outside the country, with, as its founding moment, General de Gaulle's Appeal of June 18, 1940, broadcast over the radio from London; and also inside France itself, with the banding together of the first Resistance groups and networks.

Resistance takes many forms: providing information to the Allies; sabotage; distributing leaflets, songs, and secret magazines and newspapers; passive resistance; helping Jews in hiding; armed struggle; even hastily scrawled graffiti—*anti-collabo* or pro-Allied slogans. There are as many instances of informal, occasional resistance as of active, organized Resistance.

The first contacts between the Free French government in exile in London and the Resistance movements in France take place in late 1941; after that, these two sides of the French Resistance will work together through the end of the war. The numerous groups that form at first in both the Northern Zone of Occupation and in the Free Zone controlled by Vichy will, little by little, join forces, thanks to the work of agents sent from England. A few months after the invasion of the south by the German army (following Allied landings in North Africa), Jean Moulin founds, in May 1943, the National Council of the Resistance. >>>

A portrait of Jean Moulin in 1939. He was at the time prefect (governor of a *département*) of Eure-et-Loir. He will make his way to London in 1941 and parachute onto French soil in January 1942 on orders from General de Gaulle, tasked with unifying the various Resistance movements.
© BAVCC

A Maquis band in the *département* of Ain in the Rhône-Alpes marches through the city of Oyonnax, November 11, 1943.
Caen Memorial

L'Avant-Garde, the newspaper published by the Jeunesses Communistes Françaises (the French Communist youth league), went underground during the war to aid the cause of the Resistance.
Caen Memorial

The notorious Affiche Rouge (Red Poster) was part of a major propaganda campaign by Vichy French and German authorities in spring 1944 in occupied Paris aimed at discrediting the Resistance network led by Missak Manouchian, 23 of whose 100 or so fighters, most of them immigrants, were executed in 1944.
Caen Memorial

>>> Starting in early 1943, the Resistance benefits from a massive influx of men who refuse to be press-ganged into the Obligatory Work Service, a program put in place by Pierre Laval, head of the Vichy government, that involved sending young French workers to Germany in exchange for the return of French prisoners of war as part of Laval's policy of collaboration. The Maquis groups form: bands of armed Resistance fighters hiding in the forests or the mountains, first in the Vercors highlands (starting in 1942), and later on the Glière plateau in Haute-Savoie, in the French Alps (starting in January 1944).

The Resistance plays an important role in the lead-up to D-Day through acts of sabotage and espionage. After Liberation, many members of the Resistance, the bulk of whom regroup as the French Forces of the Interior (FFI), help the Allies drive the Germans out.

The risks undertaken by those in the Resistance throughout the war vary according their degree of involvement: in some cases, those risks include prison, torture, death by firing squad, or deportation. Moreover, acts of resistance provoke reprisals by the Nazis, who regularly hold civilians hostage and execute them. ●

The Resistance fighter Marcel Maillard wrote letters on cigarette rolling papers during his imprisonment in Fresnes, near Paris, where members of the Resistance and British agents were held by the Nazis in horrific conditions, tortured, and executed. Maillard was shot with 19 fellow detainees on April 11, 1944.
Caen Memorial

The singer Anna Marly (1917–2006) wrote the "Chant du Partisans" (Song of the Partisans), the Resistance's most famous tune. Marly's original lyrics were in her native Russian; French lyrics were devised in London in 1943 by Joseph Kessel and Maurice Druon.
Caen Memorial

World War— Total War

By Pierre Laborie

Jewish Soviet partisans are hanged in Minsk, October 26, 1941. Masha Ruskina, age 17, is at left.
© Ria Novosti

Soviet infantry mount
an attack in the USSR,
November 1941.
© Magnum / Dimitri Baltermants

From European War to World War

The Context

In the 1930s, all over the world, authoritarian regimes made threats, outright provocation, and military fait accompli their tactics of first resort, in defiance of treaties and international law. Japan in Manchuria, Italy in Ethiopa, and Germany in Italy and Spain all intervened in regional conflicts and civil wars.

These clashes functioned as testing grounds in both military and diplomatic terms. In the face of such acts of aggression and military strikes, the European democracies only revealed their blindness. Deeply scarred by the slaughter and sacrifice of World War I, they opposed the fascist threats with nothing but their longing for peace. Nonetheless, it is simplistic to claim that war was inevitable.

Starting in the 1930s, under its "Greater East Asia" policy of colonial expansion, Japan ruled the territories it conquered by installing new national governments that were in fact entirely controlled from Tokyo. The first of these puppet regimes was set up in Manchuria in 1932 with the creation of Manchukuo with the deposed Chinese emperor as nominal head of state—a pattern Hitler would later follow across Europe.

THE TRIPARTITE PACT
The treaty that established the Axis alliance was signed on September 27, 1940 by Germany, Italy, and Japan. Most of the states allied to or controlled by the Axis powers also joined, including Bulgaria, Hungary, Finland, the Republic of China (that is, Nanjing after the collapse of the Qing dynasty) under President Wang Jingwei, and Manchukuo.

JAPANESE-SOVIET NONAGGRESSION PACT
On April 13, 1941 the USSR and Japan sign a treaty of neutrality, which will remain in force until August 8, 1945, when the Red Army invades Manchuria, two days after the bombing of Hiroshima.

THE NEAR AND MIDDLE EAST
In order to prevent Germany from expanding into the eastern Mediterranean and gaining access to its oil wells, the British invade Iraq. Together with the Free French Forces (the Forces Françaises Libres, or FFL), the British also occupy Vichy French–controlled Syria and Lebanon in June–July 1941.

FRANCE
In spring 1942, as the Wehrmacht's success seems to demonstrate the invincibility of Hitler's war machine, Vichy prime minister Pierre Laval expresses his hope for a German victory and expands the policy of collaboration.

Puyi, the last Qing emperor of China, is installed by the Japanese as the head of state of occupied Manchukuo in 1932 and declared emperor with the era name of Kangde ("Tranquility and Virtue") in 1934.
© Suddeutsche Zeitung / Rue des Archives

British soldiers outside Baghdad, April 30, 1941.
© Imperial War Museum

The Tripartite Pact is signed by the Nazi foreign minister, Joachim von Ribbentrop, the Japanese ambassador to Germany, Saburo Kurusu, and the Italian foreign minister, Count Galeazzo Ciano, before Hitler in Berlin on September 27, 1940.
© Rue des Archives / Tal

From European War to World War

The Japanese surprise attack on Pearl Harbor on December 7, 1941, at last draws the U.S. into the war. Invoking the Tripartite Pact, Germany and Italy declare war on the U.S. four days later. The U.S. entry into the war and Japanese offensives in the Pacific confirm the global dimensions of the conflict: on land, at sea, and in the air, in multiple, simultaneous theaters of battle, and involving vast forces on a scale unprecedented in human history. Only a few months earlier, in June 1941, the German invasion of the Soviet Union had terminated the German–Soviet nonaggression pact, opening up a new eastern front in the European war. The evolving conflict accelerates the radical transformation of the methods of making war that is already under way, altering irreversibly the nature of armed conflict.

A German-made globe, 1943.
Caen Memorial

THE MILITARY SITUATION, AUTUMN 1940– AUTUMN 1941

In the fall of 1940, Mussolini invades Greece; the operation ends in a stinging defeat. In spring 1941, Germany takes over in the Balkans, occupying Greece and Yugoslavia. Alone in Europe against Nazi Germany, Britain must rely on American aid, sent by ship across the Atlantic. German U-boats sink more and more Allied shipping—2.5 million metric tons in 1941. In North Africa, the advance of the Italian army is blocked by British and Commonwealth forces throughout winter 1940–41. In February 1941, Hitler sends General Erwin Rommel into Libya to reinforce the Italians. Rommel reconquers the lost territory for the Axis, except for the city of Tobruk, with its important port. On June 22, 1941, the German army invades the USSR, ending the German–Soviet pact. The Germans conquer the Baltic countries, then lay siege to Leningrad. German victory at Smolensk opens the way to Moscow. In the south, the German offensive in Ukraine ends with the sieges of the Black Sea ports of Odessa and Sebastopol. In the Middle East, Germany and the Allies vie for influence. In May 1941, Britain continues to hold Iraq; in June and July, the British invade Syria. In September, the Soviets and the British both occupy Iran.

General Bernard Montgomery at the battle of El Alamein in Egypt, November 1942.
© Imperial War Museum

The Widening War

After the fall of France in May and June 1940, the war widens in waves that spread across the European continent, soon reaching Greece and Yugoslavia. The Allies and the Axis also fight for dominance in the air and at sea to maintain their supply lines. The Battle of the Atlantic rages in autumn 1940.

At the same time, as the opposing forces fight for control of the Mediterranean and the Suez Canal, the war spreads to include North Africa and the Middle East.

The failure of the Italian offensive in Egypt in autumn 1940 compels Germany to confront the British in North Africa. In June 1942, after several attempts, Rommel's Afrikakorps reaches the coastal town of El Alamein in Egypt. British General Bernard Montgomery takes command of the 8th Army's combined British, Commonwealth, Greek, and Free French Forces (FFL) . ■

General Erwin Rommel,
commander of the
Afrikakorps, and Italian
general Giorgio, Count Calvi
di Bergolo, prepare to attack
the port of Tobruk in Libya,
December 12, 1941.
© Keystone-France / Eyedea Presse

**The participation of the
Free French forces** under
General Marie-Pierre
Koenig in the North African
campaign marked the return
of the French army to battle
for the first time since the
fall of France. Libya, 1942.
© ECPAD

**A column of German
armored vehicles** destroyed
by South African troops in
Libya, January 1942.
© Associated Press

The Invasion of the USSR

The Wehrmacht invades the USSR on June 22, 1941. By autumn, the Germans and their allies (Finnish, Romanian, Hungarian, Italian, Slovak, and Croatian troops) occupy an immense expanse of territory. They halt their advance outside Leningrad and Moscow for the winter—without having attained their objectives— and resume the offensive in 1942.

While the entry of the U.S. and Japan into the war gives the conflict its global dimension, it is the German invasion of the USSR that irrevocably changes its nature. On the Eastern Front, World War II becomes a mass slaughter beyond all imagining. ■

Soviet prisoners of war
captured during the battle of Kharkov, USSR, May 1942.
© BPK

Both the German and Soviet armies adopt scorched-earth tactics to reduce each other's ability to resupply their troops, Ukraine, 1942.
© BPK

German infantrymen pass through a fleet of abandoned Soviet military vehicles and other matériel, USSR, 1941.
© Ullstein Bild / SV Bilderdie

A column of German tanks crosses the Ukrainian plains, USSR, 1941.
© BPK

A village in flames, USSR, 1941–42.
© Signal / Caen Memorial

For Hitler, the invasion of the USSR, dubbed Operation Barbarossa, is at once a war of conquest for *Lebensraum* ("living space"), an ideological war, and a war of racial annihilation directed against the menace of "Judeo-Bolshevism."

A German propaganda unit vehicle equipped with loudspeakers encourages Soviet troops to surrender, USSR, ca. 1941–42.
© Signal / Caen Memorial

Soviet military losses in summer 1941 are colossal: 1.5 million dead and 4 million prisoners; some 2.8 million of the latter will die within the next eight months, killed by starvation, exposure, and summary execution.
© BPK

The Enigma M4 coding
machine used by the
Kriegsmarine, the German
navy. Germany, 1943.
Collection of the Norwegian
Armed Forces Museum, Oslo

The War in the Atlantic and the Atlantic Charter

The Battle of the Atlantic

German submarines attack in the Atlantic, especially in the "black hole" (an initially vast area where ships could not be protected by air cover, which would be gradually reduced over the course of the war with improvements in aviation), inflicting heavy losses on convoys of vital importance to Great Britain.

The fight for control of the Suez Canal and Mediterranean shipping lanes leads to the opening of a new front in North Africa.

American Wartime Politics

Despite opposition from isolationist Republicans, the American Lend-Lease program is passed into law in March 1941, authorizing the "loan" of war matériel and other strategic supplies to countries whose defense is judged vital to American security. (Supplies that are not destroyed will later be sold to Britain at a discount using long-term U.S. loans; these loans, and similar loans from Canada, will not be fully repaid until 2006). The principle beneficiaries of Lend-Lease are Great Britain and the USSR, starting in summer 1941; Greece, France, and China also receive aid. The program forms the foundation of what will be called the Grand Alliance.

The Atlantic Charter results from the meeting between Churchill and U.S. president Franklin D. Roosevelt aboard a warship off the Newfoundland coast, August 9–12, 1941. Four months before the official entry of the U.S. into the war, the charter states the Allies' ideal goals and principles, including no acquisition of territory or changes of borders against the wishes of the peoples involved, restoration of self-government to conquered peoples, access to raw materials and reduction of trade restrictions, freedom of the seas, and abandonment of the use of force and disarmament of aggressor nations. ∎

Roosevelt and Churchill with their staff officers off the coast of Newfoundland, August 1941.
© National Archives

Le Courrier de l'Air, a publication produced in Britain to counter German propaganda in occupied Europe and dropped by the RAF behind enemy lines, announces the Atlantic Charter.
Caen Memorial

A merchant ship is struck by a torpedo, June 1941.
© Signal / Caen Memorial

A British cargo ship sinks, victim of a German U-boat, in June 1941.
© Signal / Caen Memorial

Japanese Expansionism

By 1941, Japan is able to draw upon sufficient military resources to assure its superiority over other western Pacific regional powers despite its economic dependence on imported U.S. oil and other commodities. Some Japanese leaders persuade themselves that Japan could win a war against the U.S., if victory were to come swiftly enough. Faced with determined American opposition to its policy of expansion in Asia, Japan puts an end to negotiations with the U.S. with a wholly unanticipated military strike. On December 7, 1941, without an official

The buun-tchokyu, a patriotic good-luck flag inscribed by family and friends with prayers for honor and good fortune, was a standard part of every Japanese soldier's kit. This one is in silk, ca. 1940–45.
Caen Memorial

The Japanese fleet becomes the main instrument for implementing Japan's imperialist strategy. Photo shot in Japanese waters, ca. 1935–38.
© Der Adler / Caen Memorial

declaration of war, the Japanese navy launches an air and submarine raid against the U.S. Pacific Fleet docked in Pearl Harbor, Hawaii, more than 3,000 miles from the Japanese coast. Conceived by Admiral Isoroku Yamamoto and led by Admiral Chūichi Nagumo, the surprise attack inflicts heavy losses: 2,400 dead and 1,300 wounded, with most of the U.S. fleet sunk or damaged.

Following this lightning offensive, within months Japan establishes its domination over most of the islands and peninsulas of the Pacific in Southeast Asia. Only in New Guinea (then administered by Australia) do the Japanese meet with any real opposition. India and Australia—both, as Commonwealth nations, bastions of the Allied war effort—are now threatened.

Many scholars will try to understand how this "date which will live in infamy," as Roosevelt calls it, could have arrived. Some historians have proposed that Roosevelt deliberately pro-voked the Japanese by imposing economic sanctions, freezing Japanese assets in the U.S., and cutting off trade, including oil exports. Others have claimed that the Roosevelt administration had advance knowledge of the attack, but ignored it to secure public and Congressional support for joining the Allied war effort, or even that Pearl Harbor was left exposed to attack in order to force American entry into the war. However, no conclusive evidence supports these hypotheses.

Undertaken ostensibly in the name of a struggle against European colonialism, the Japanese campaigns at first take advantage of support from local nationalist movements. Yet the protracted and intensifying conflict changes the picture, as the colonial protectorates of East Asia are transformed by Japanese conquest into occupied countries, entirely controlled by and forced to endure the harsh demands of the Japanese war machine. ∎

Japanese infantry massed outside a Chinese city, March 1941.
© L'Illustration

Honolulu Star-Bulletin 1st EXTRA

8 PAGES - HONOLULU, TERRITORY OF HAWAII, U.S.A. SUNDAY, DECEMBER 7, 1941 - 8 PAGES ★ PRICE FIVE CENTS

(Associated Press by Transpacific Telephone)

SAN FRANCISCO, Dec. 7.—President Roosevelt announced this morning that Japanese planes had attacked Manila and Pearl Harbor.

WAR!
OAHU BOMBED BY JAPANESE PLANES

The battleships USS *Tennessee* and USS *West Virginia* are badly damaged. The latter sinks, but both will be repaired, modernized, and returned to service. The USS *Arizona* sinks and is today a national memorial. Sailors in small craft attempt to rescue survivors. Pearl Harbor, December 7, 1941.
© National Archives

Roosevelt declares war on Japan on December 7, 1941, after the attack on Pearl Harbor.
© Rue des Archives / Tal

Personnel at the Naval Air Station on Ford Island clean up the runway after the Japanese attack. In the background, the destroyer USS *Shaw* explodes in flames. Pearl Harbor, December 7, 1941.
© Associated Press

A group of Stormtroopers humiliates a German Christian and her Jewish friend in Cuxhaven, on the German coast near Denmark, on July 27, 1933. The rhymes on the placards read:

I am the biggest sow in town; For Jews only I'll go down!

A Jewish boy, I've always led German girls to my bed!

© Yad Vashem

Genocide
and Mass
Violence

The annual Nazi Party Congress, Nuremberg, 1936.
Caen Memorial

Genocide and Mass Violence: The Extermination of Jews in Europe

The war years are marked by mass killings and countless atrocities. At the center of the collective murder, the extermination of European Jews is not merely another massacre, but an historical event whose unprecedented significance is inconceivable at the time—a period in which, above all, common decency is overwhelmed by indifference.

The uniqueness of the Shoah lies not only in the monstrousness of the Nazis' killing methods or in the number of victims, but also in their will to murder, their determination to make a group of human beings disappear in its entirety by eliminating any possibility of survival for their descendents. Hence, the methodical slaughter of Jewish mothers and their children. However, while the singularity of the Shoah among crimes against humanity must not be denied, its history is nonetheless inseparable from its context: the eruption of barbarity and extreme violence that characterize World War II.

The diary of Berthe Auroy, a retired French primary school teacher, which she keeps from 1940 to 1944. On this page, Berthe notes, "Jews must wear the yellow star starting on June 7. On the left side of the chest and all those over six years of age."
Caen Memorial

A streetcar in Warsaw reserved for Jews, Poland, October 1940.
© Bundesarchiv

According to Hitler's plan, the "living space" that the Germans would conquer in Eastern Europe must be *Judenfrei*, "free of Jews." Hitler needed to find a "solution" to the "Jewish question," and many possibilities were proposed before the adoption of the Final Solution.

THE SHOAH BY BULLETS

The ravine at Babi Yar in Ukraine, where 33,771 Jews were killed on September 28–29, 1941, has become one of the symbols of the martyrdom of Jewish communities in the former USSR. The countless massacres in every German-occupied country, often with the participation of local militias, testify to the frenzy of racial violence that typifies the war in Eastern Europe.

Continuing the pioneering work on the mass murder of Jews by the *Einsatzgruppen* (paramilitary task forces), such as Raul Hilberg's *The Destruction of the European Jews* (1961), research groups directed by Father Patrick Desbois have undertaken extensive investigations in Ukraine. They have uncovered more than 600 sites where thousands of Jews were buried after having been shot—"the Shoah by bullets."

A METHODICAL PLAN FOR EXTERMINATION

By the end of the war, of the 3.35 million Jews estimated to have been living in Poland in 1939, 90 percent had been exterminated. In Romania, historians estimate that more than 350,000 Romanian and Ukranian Jews were exterminated by the Romanian army and gendarmes without any direct, active participation by Nazi Germany. Among the many atrocities often overlooked, the massacre of the 48,000 Jewish inmates of the Bogdanovka concentration camp in Romania in 1941 stands out for its speed and cruelty.

The German "total war" effort consumed vast resources, and in particular made enormous demands on labor, including slave labor; the labor force devoted to war production is estimated at 4 million. Nonetheless, the Nazis continued their campaign of mass murder of Jews until the very last days of the war, for example in Hungary, whose Jewish community was not deported and killed until 1944–45.

WHAT DID THE ALLIES KNOW?

In August 1942, Gerhart Giegner sent the Allies a telegram on behalf of the World Jewish Congress in Geneva, informing them of the existence of a plan to exterminate millions of Jews, based on information from the German industrialist Eduard Schulte. Yet Giegner failed to convince either British or American authorities. The information was considered too outrageous to be credible, and the Allied military leaders had other priorities. While premonitions of the worst seem to have been very widespread, owing to the Nazis' well-known persecution of the Jews, the existence of a planned program of extermination was not clearly grasped until after the war. The reality of the genocide, and its unique character, enters the collective consciousness only much later.

Young Parisians rush through the entrance to an amusement park in 1941. The sign reads INTERDIT AUX JUIFS: "Off-limits to Jews."
© CDJC / Fonds Urman

SS Unterscharführer Johann Gorges, an SS junior squad leader who worked at the Auschwitz-Birkenau death camp, is shown in this drawing killing a camp inmate. Gorges was indicted for crimes against humanity after the war, but died in 1971 before his prosecution could begin.
© Ghetto Fighters' House—Itzhak Katzenelson Holocaust and Jewish Resistance Heritage Museum, Israel

"The gas chambers, the industrial slaughter of human beings, no, I confess, I did not imagine them, and because I could not imagine them, I did not know about them."
Raymond Aron

The **Rayman family,** Poland, 1929.
© Mémorial de la Shoah / CDJC

The Shoah

The uniqueness of the Jewish genocide lies in the nature of the crime, in the professed aim of total annihilation, in the methods selected to achieve that goal, and in the "racial" criterion for the killing, regardless of age or sex.

For the Nazis, the Jews represented a primordial menace. In their eyes, the Jews threatened the biological survival and even the very existence of the German nation.

The details of the methodical destruction of Jews across Europe—where and when and how it was accomplished—are well known today. However, widespread public acceptance of the reality of the Shoah after the war was slowed by the difficulty of comprehending a truth whose monstrous dimensions seemed literally inconceivable to those who lived with the war. ∎

THE MILITARY SITUATION, SPRING 1942

Spring 1942 marks the apex of Axis power and success. A series of spectacular victories gives Japan mastery of the Pacific. Germany launches new offensives in the USSR, while, in North Africa, a combined German–Italian army reaches the outskirts of Alexandria. On January 18, 1942, in Berlin, the Axis powers sign a military accord that extends the terms of the Tripartite Pact, establishing their respective geographical areas of operation. Directly or indirectly, most of the world's people now find themselves involved in the war. Starting in 1942, the map of the globe must be continually redrawn to represent the shifting zones of influence resulting from the changing military situation and each country's relation to the two opposing coalitions, the Allies and the Axis.　　**>>>**

Jews are forced to march through the streets of Baden-Baden, carrying a large yellow star. Germany, 1938. © BPK

The Final Solution

Historians were long divided in maintaining so-called *intentionalist* or *functionalist* explanations of the origins of the Final Solution. Intentionalists contend that the Nazis decided to exterminate the Jews long before the Final Solution. Functionalists counter that the atrocities resulted less from Hitler's orders than from an autonomous process, a series of improvised responses to local circumstances, without any preconceived plan or program.

As an expansion of the mass killings effected by the *Einsatzgruppen*, the decision to exterminate the Jews of Europe was without question taken by late autumn 1941. The logistical aspects were dealt with at the Wannsee Conference on January 20, 1942. The Final Solution was in effect conceived as a rationalized process, an industrialization of death, planned and developed at the very highest levels of the Nazi hierarchy. It was implemented methodically, with stubborn insistence, even to the detriment of German strategic interests, as a goal independent of the Nazis' overall war aims. ■

The War in Europe
Spring 1943

■ Axis countries and their allies
■ Territories under Axis control
■ Territories under Vichy control
■ Allied countries
■ Territories under Allied control
　Neutral countries
— Borders of the Third Reich
— The Eastern Front, spring 1942
▨ Territories reconquered by the USSR, winter 1941–42

Black smoke rises over the Hadamar Euthanasia Center, where the bodies of Jews who had been gassed are incinerated in a crematorium oven. Urns containing the ashes of the victims were sent back to their families with falsified death certificates. Germany, ca. 1939–41.
© Hessisches Hauptstaatsarchiv Wiesbaden

The War in the Pacific
Spring 1943

■ Japanese Empire, 1931	■ Allied countries and territories under Allied control
■ Territories under Japanese control before December 7, 1941	■ Allied countries that have not declared war on Japan
■ Territories conquered by Japan	☐ Neutral countries
	— The Pacific Front, spring 1942

ACTION T4: THE NAZI EUTHANASIA PROGRAM

The Nazis adopted the code T4 to designate the elimination by euthanasia of the physically and mentally handicapped in Germany. The decision to begin the program, which was undertaken in the name of a policy of "social hygiene," was made in summer 1939. Between 70,000 and 90,000 people were exterminated before the operation was officially ended in August 1941, ostensibly in response to objections from the German churches. (Research in files recovered after 1990 shows that the program continued secretly until 1945 and that at least 200,000 were killed.) Action T4 enabled the Nazis to experiment with various execution methods, including gassing with carbon monoxide. In autumn 1941, specialists from the T4 program were sent to Poland to prepare the extermination facilities at the Belzec and Sobibor death camps, shortly before the opening of the Treblinka camp.

>>> The borders of the resulting territorial divisions will change ceaselessly as events unfold. In Europe, Iceland, Sweden, Ireland, Switzerland, and Portugal declare themselves neutral, as does Turkey. Despite its official neutrality, Franco's Spain supports the cause of the Reich before distancing itself from the Axis starting in 1943. In 1942, most of the Latin American republics side with the Allies, though they vary in their degrees of support. Only Chile and Argentina decline, for the time being, to break off relations with the Axis countries. Chile will do so in January 1943, Argentina in January 1944.

The female personnel at the Hadamar Euthanasia Center, where some 10,000 people were killed. Germany, ca. 1939–41.
© Hessisches Hauptstaatsarchiv Wiesbaden

A yellow star stamped JUDE, "Jew." German, 1941.
Caen Memorial

From Persecution to Extermination

The process of exterminating the Jews of Europe did not unfold everywhere according to a single pattern or chronology, nor in any mechanical sequence of identical phases, nor at the same time. It took different forms in each country, according to their histories and circumstances in the war. In Ukraine, for example, mass executions by shooting followed immediately upon the forced assembly of the Jews in each community. By contrast, it was only late in the war, in spring 1944, that more than 450,000 Hungarian Jews were deported to Auschwitz-Birkenau in an intensive campaign that lasted only 56 days. ■

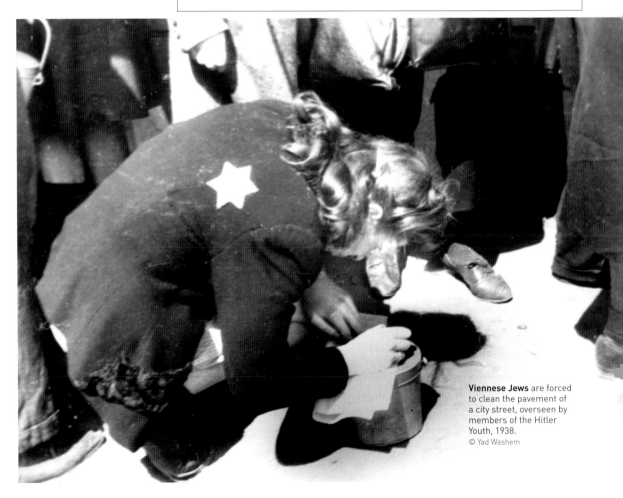

Viennese Jews are forced to clean the pavement of a city street, overseen by members of the Hitler Youth, 1938.
© Yad Washem

The Statute on Jews published by the Vichy government in 1941.
Caen Memorial

A German Jew sits on a bench designated NUR FÜR JUDEN: "For Jews Only." Germany, ca. 1933–45.
© Yad Vashem

An illustration from the cover of an anti-Semitic brochure entitled *Youpino* (Kike-y), France, ca. 1941–44.
Caen Memorial

A French identity card stamped JEW that belonged to Alphonse Cerf, then aged 17.
Yad Vashem Artifacts Collection, Gift of Alphonse Cerf, Israel

"*Today I will once more be a prophet. If the international Jewish financiers in and outside Europe should succeed in plunging the nations once more into a world war, then the result will not be the bolshevization of the earth, and thus the victory of Jewry, but the annihilation of the Jewish race in Europe!*"

Adolf Hitler, Speech to the Reichstag, January 30, 1939

Hungarian Jewish women under arrest, summer 1944.
© AKG-images

A Jewish couple reading a notice posted by the Nazi government, Germany, February 1941.
© Bundesarchiv

THE GHETTOS

Together with the concentration camps (such as Dachau, Buchenwald, Ravensbrück, and Sachsenhausen-Oranienburg) and the extermination or death camps (such as Auschwitz-Birkenau, Treblinka, Belsec, and Sobibor), the ghettos, which numbered more than 400, formed the third main element in the Nazi archipelago of mass murder. Each ghetto generally occupied a very small neighborhood within a big city (such as Warsaw, Łódź, Vilna, or Kovno); some were even restricted to a single very large building. The ghettos were surrounded by walls at least ten feet high topped by barbed wire. There tens or hundreds of thousands of Jews from the big cities of Eastern Europe were confined, together with others transported from their homes in small towns, villages, and the countryside. Designed to collect the Jews together and imprison them—indeed, to corral and suffocate them—the ghettos also served to sever every link between the Jewish communities and their broader social environment, to cut off all material support, all means of communication, all human relationships with non-Jews. Ostensibly governed by the *Judenräte* or "Jewish councils" (municipal administrations set up by the Nazis), the ghettos, with their extreme squalor, filth, epidemic disease, and deliberately inflicted starvation, were in effect mere way stations on the road to death. For the Nazis, the ghettos from the beginning never represented anything more than a temporary stop on the way to deportation and execution.

In the Łódź ghetto children pull a cart loaded with huge sacks, Poland, ca. 1940–44. Photo courtesy of the Ghetto Fighters' House—Itzhak Katzenelson Holocaust and Jewish Resistance Heritage Museum, Israel

ABOVE, UPPER: **These fifteen mass graves** near the Busk commune, in the Lvov region, Ukraine, were excavated by a team led by Father Patrick Desbois in August 2006.
© Guillaume Ribot

ABOVE, LOWER: **Skeletons exhumed** from grave 17 lie jumbled together, Busk, Ukraine, 2006.
© Guillaume Ribot

RIGHT: **Lithuanian Jews are executed** by an *Einsatzkommando* (a small subgroup of an *Einsatzgruppe*—a mobile extermination squad), 1941.
© Ria Novosti

Shell casings dating from ca. 1941–44, found at the edges of mass graves in Ukraine.
© Collection of Yahad–In Unum

Extermination at Close Range

Although the extermination camps at Auschwitz-Birkenau, Belzec, Chelmno, Treblinka, Sobibor, and Majdanek remain the most essential "sites of memory" (to use historian Pierre Nora's term), recent research highlights the significant contribution of close-range extermination to the total number of victims.

Of the 6 million dead, between 1.5 and 2 million Jews were not gassed, but shot.

This fact testifies to the deliberate process of desensitization used to train the *Einsatzgruppen*, to the killers' relentlessness, and to the complicity in some countries of non-Jewish citizens who were witnesses and often participants in the slaughter. Analysis of the Nazis' killing methods prior to setting up the death camps compels us to reevaluate the familiar concept of the Shoah as an abstract bureaucratic process, a secret industry of genocide. ∎

"So I joined in the great slaughter the day before yesterday. With the first vehicles (which brought the victims), my hand shook at the moment of firing, but you get used to it. By the tenth, I was aiming calmly and shooting with a steady hand—women, children, and infants. I had in mind the fact that I also have two infants at home, and that this pack of wild animals would have acted in exactly the same way with them, maybe even ten times worse. The death we gave them was gentle and quick compared to the infernal tortures endured by the thousands and thousands of people in the prisons of the Communist secret police. The infants flew through the sky in big arcs and we shot them in midair before they fell into the pit or in the water. We have to finish off these beasts that have dragged Europe into war."

Letter from an Austrian policeman to his wife, written on October 5, 1941, after the liquidation of a ghetto in Byelorussia

Roundup of the Jews of Lubny, Ukraine, shortly before their massacre by units of the *Einsatzgruppen*, October 16, 1941.
© Yad Vashem

Members of an *Einsatzkommando* shoot Jews in a field near Dubossary, Moldova, on September 14, 1941.
© USHMM, Imperial War Museum

Jewish families waiting to enter the gas chamber, Auschwitz-Birkenau, May 1944. © AKG-images

Jewish women and children waiting in the birch forest that conceals the crematoria at the Auschwitz-Birkenau death camp in Poland, May 26, 1944. © Yad Vashem

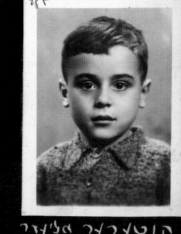

Children in the Shoah

Of the 4,918 children deported to Auschwitz from Belgium, 53 returned. Of the 15,000 children who passed through Theresienstadt (Terezín), which the Nazis built as a "show ghetto" or "show camp" to prove to international organizations such as the Red Cross how well Jews lived under their benevolent regime, about 100 survived. Of the 11,400 children deported from France, only 200, all adolescents, returned home.

Six million European Jews disappeared during the Shoah. Among them, 1,250,000 children, or nine in ten, were murdered, by the cruelest means possible. When the Nazi regime fell, no more than 100,000 to 120,000 Jewish children survived in all of Europe, or 6 to 11 percent of the prewar total, principally in the West. In entire regions of Central and Eastern Europe, there remained not a single living Jewish child.

Those who survived, many of them orphans, had moreover to suffer the psychological isolation of those unable to make others understand what they have endured. In the words of the Austrian-born Resistance fighter, death camp survivor, and essayist Jean Améry, they had to try to live normally despite being "deprived of trust in the world." ∎

Photos of children from the Koordinacja album. The Koordinacja was an association that tried to locate and care for the hundreds of Polish children who had survived the Shoah in Poland and attempted to reunite them with their families if possible, and to care for Jewish orphans. This album was created by Hella Leneman, who ran the Koordinacja's children's home in Łódź.
Ghetto Fighters' House—Itzhak Katzenelson Holocaust and Jewish Resistance Heritage Museum, Israel, gift of Hella Leneman

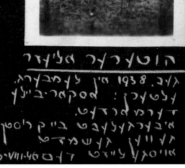

A bookbag that belonged to Roger Stern, a Jewish boy deported to Auschwitz with his brother, André, and their parents on transport 64 from the Drancy internment camp near Paris on December 7, 1943.
Dépôt Mémorial de la Shoah / CDJC (Paris), Stern-Gaillard Collection

The Extermination Camps

Estimates of the number of Jewish victims in the main camps and extermination centers.

Chelmno *Opened in December 1941*	**150,000–220,000**
Belzec *Opened in March 1942*	**435,000–600,000**
Sobibor *Opened in April 1942*	**150,000–250,000**
Treblinka *Opened in July 1942*	**800,000–950,000**
Auschwitz-Birkenau *Fully operational in spring 1942*	**1,000,000**
Majdanek *Opened in October 1941; becomes death camp with gas chambers in October 1942*	**80,000–200,000**

The Extermination Camps in Poland

SWEDEN

REICHSKOMMISSARIAT OSTLAND

Vilnius

Dantzig

Białystok

Berlin
Chelmno   Treblinka   Brest-Litovsk
GERMANY   Warsaw
Łódź   Sobibor   REICHSKOMMISSARIAT UKRAINE
Majdanek

Belzec

Auschwitz-   GENERAL GOVERNMENT
Birkenau   OF POLAND
Prague   Krakow   Lvov
PROTECTORATE OF
BOHEMIA-MORAVIA

SLOVAKIA
Tchernovtsy
Vienna   Bratislava
HUNGARY   ROMANIA

The Third Reich
Areas within the Reich with special status
Other Axis countries
Territories occupied by the Axis
Neutral countries
Borders in: —— 1942
----- 1938

The entrance to the Auschwitz extermination camp.
National Archives

Crematorium III at Auschwitz.
The medical vehicle visible in the foreground delivered attending SS doctors and Zyklon B, the cyanide-based pesticide used in the gas chambers.
Ghetto Fighters' House—Itzhak Katzenelson Holocaust and Jewish Resistance Heritage Museum, Israel

Member of a *Sonderkommando* salvaging food from belongings left in the undressing room.
Ghetto Fighters' House—Itzhak Katzenelson Holocaust and Jewish Resistance Heritage Museum, Israel

The Sonderkommandos

In the death camps, some deportees, mostly Jews, were assigned to separate "special units" and forced to carry out the final stages of the extermination process: transporting and stripping the corpses after gassing, then burning them in ovens or in open pits. Sometimes called the "living dead" of the camps, they were periodically liquidated and replaced. No trace of the Nazis' crimes was supposed to remain. Yet it is to them that we owe some of the most important evidence: a few handwritten texts recovered from the mud and ash of Auschwitz-Birkenau. Attempted revolts by *Sonderkommando* members there on October 6–7, 1944, ended in a bloodbath, and fewer than ninety of the thousand at that camp survived the war. ■

The cremation of the bodies of gassed camp inmates photographed secretly from the interior of the Crematorium V gas chamber at Auschwitz-Birkenau by an unidentified member of the Polish resistance movement in Auschwitz, August 1944.
© APM Oświęcim

The crematorium oven room. An elevator visible in the background brought up the bodies from the basement, where the gas chamber was located.
© Yad Vashem

The Roma and Sinti

In Germany, as in other European countries, the Roma and Sinti (both commonly called Gypsies) were an ethnically diverse but widely despised group, often considered antisocial and hereditarily criminal.

Like German Jews, German Roma/Sinti were excluded as a "foreign and inferior race" from the national community, or *Volksgemeinschaft*, by the Nuremberg Laws of 1935. In order to protect "Aryan" racial purity, sexual relations and marriage between "Aryans" and "Gypsies" (or Jews) were forbidden. Nonetheless, some 10 percent of the German Roma/Sinti were classified as "pure Gypsies," considered "Aryan," and entitled to preferential treatment. ∎

Roma/Sinti in the Belzec extermination camp in Poland in 1942.
© AKG-images

A Forgotten Genocide

The campaign to eradicate the "Gypsy plague" began in 1938. Later, several thousand were deported from Germany to Poland in May 1940 and confined within the Łódź ghetto, where many died from starvation and epidemic disease. The survivors were gassed at Chelmno in 1942.

In December 1942, 23,000 Roma/Sinti of many nationalities (German, Czech, Polish, and others, including 145 French citizens) were deported to Auschwitz-Birkenau and grouped together in the "family camp." They were forced to wear the black triangle, for antisocials. Many of the children were used as guinea pigs for the horrific medical experiments directed by Dr. Joseph Mengele, the medical officer of Auschwitz-Birkenau's "Gypsy camp." When this camp was closed, all the nearly 3,000 Roma/Sinti still alive were gassed on August 3–4, 1944, including all the women and children.

Of the Roma/Sinti imprisoned at Auschwitz-Birkenau, about 20 percent were gassed, while more than 60 percent (14,000–15,000) died of disease and maltreatment. The remaining 20 percent were transferred to concentration camps.

The Nazi deportation and extermination of the Roma/Sinti were not in fact the main causes of the slaughter that devastated their communities throughout Europe. Many were killed at home in circumstances that varied widely from country to country.

Various aspects of the persecution of the Roma/Sinti echo the Shoah, and genocidal massacres of both peoples took place in many parts of Europe. There are limits to this analogy, however. According to Nazi ideology, the Roma/Sinti and the Jews did not have the same status. The "Gypsies" represented a "plague" against which Germany had to protect itself by preventive measures, but they were not identified as a mortal threat, an absolute enemy to be destroyed. Their extermination was not systematic, nor did it originate solely in the Nazis' racial policies. Because many of the local massacres of Roma/Sinti remain little known and poorly understood, estimates range widely, from 50,000 to 200,000 deaths, depending upon the sources consulted and the data available. ∎

ABOVE, UPPER:
Anthropologist Eva Justin takes anthropometric measurements of a Roma/Sinti woman, Germany, 1938.
© Bundesarchiv / Schilf

ABOVE, LOWER: **Roma/Sinti communities in Germany** were examined by the Reich's Racial Hygiene and Criminal Biology and Research Unit (part of the National Ministry of Health) from 1936 to 1940.
© Bundesarchiv

Roma/Sinti deportees interned at the Ravensbrück concentration camp, Germany, ca. 1941–44.
© BPK

The bombing of the town of Guernica, in the Basque region of Spain, on April 26, 1937, by planes of the German and Italian air force allied with Franco's fascists, caused 1,654 deaths. The raid aroused an intensely emotional public response, as expressed in Pablo Picasso's famous painting *Guernica*.

The bombing of Guernica signaled a profound break with the conventional conception of war by the choice of a civilian population as the target for destruction and terror.

THE CULTURE OF WAR IN JAPAN

While claiming to seek the liberation of Southwest Asia from all Western colonial domination, the Japanese army successively annexed Taiwan in 1895, then Korea in 1910. Japanese Pan-Asianism aims to make Japan the "vital center of the world." In order to achieve this goal, the nation unites behind Emperor Hirohito, who, according to Shinto tradition, is an earthly divinity. Imbued with respect for tradition and an ancestral warrior code, Japanese soldiers are willing to sacrifice anything for victory, including their own lives. The conquest of China is viewed as the first stage in the creation of a great Japanese empire in Asia.

On December 13, 1937, five months after the beginning of the invasion of China, the Japanese army entered the city of Nanjing. The aftermath of the city's fall saw appalling carnage: execution by shooting, decapitation, drowning, stabbing, and burning alive, and an estimated 20,000 to 80,000 rapes. The hundreds of thousands of deaths during the Rape of Nanjing foreshadow the mass murders of World War II.

NAZISM AND VIOLENCE

When war begins on the Eastern Front in June 1941, according to the Nazi view of world history, Jews and communists are deeply to blame and are both identified as absolute evil. "Judeo-Bolshevism" is the enemy and represents a mortal threat. Maintaining the "purity of the Aryan race" and the very survival of Germany demand its destruction.

The savagery of the armies of the

Guernica, Spain, after bombardment by the German Luftwaffe Condor Legion and the Italian Fascist Aviazione Legionaria on April 26, 1937.
© Mary Evans / Rue des Archives

Third Reich is due in part to the harshness of conditions of the war on the Eastern Front and to the successful ideological indoctrination of the troops.

The conviction that they are engaged in a fight to the death for their own survival and the survival of Germany leads the soldiers to obey any order, to accept any atrocity, to view as "inevitable" and therefore participate in the massacre of women and children, to justify the unjustifiable.

To a lesser degree, the inhuman behavior of the German soldiers results also from the extremely severe discipline in the Wehrmacht. During World War I, 28 German soldiers were executed, compared to 650 French and 346 British troops. Between 1939 and 1945, the German army executed between 13,000 and 15,000 soldiers, an average of 200 each month, half for desertion, and half for other infractions of the military code or subversion. The objective of such harsh and repressive measures was clear: as Omer Bartov, one of the world's leading scholars of genocide, has put it, the Wehrmacht sought to terrorize soldiers tempted to escape from a probable death on the front by promising them certain death if they were recaptured after deserting. Likewise, between 1933 and 1945, German civil courts pronounced 16,500 death sentences. Virtually all were carried out.

The Nazis' mass killings did not spare Germany's own allies: nearly 6,800 Italian soldiers were liquidated by the Germans after September 1943, when the Italian army surrendered to Allied forces.

Among the most notable incidents was the mass execution of the officers and men of the Italian 33rd Acqui Infantry Division by the Wehrmacht on the island of Kefalonia, Greece, also known as the Kefalonia Massacre. Some 4,000 to 5,000 soldiers were murdered, one of the largest prisoners-of-war massacres of World War II.

Mass Violence

The term mass violence is appropriate when, in the name of winning a war, millions of human beings are annihilated deliberately and with horrific excess force—all the more so when those who adopt a policy of mass killing consider it well-founded, justified, legitimate, inevitable, and necessary.

World War I inaugurated the era of mass slaughter with the vast carnage of its battles—in which soldiers comprised most of the victims. The Battle of the Somme, for example, caused 420,000 British casualties, including 60,000 on the first day of battle alone. Such losses were at the time considered unprecedented.

The phenomenon of mass violence nonetheless reached hitherto unimaginable levels during World War II—with one major difference. This time, most often, the victims were civilians. ■

A Chinese family weeps over the death of a loved one, 1937.
© Roger Viollet

In Nanjing, China, men aged 15 to 45 were hunted down, captured, and executed.
© M. Prazan

Atrocities in Asia

Mass murder typified Imperial Japanese Army conquests throughout Asia. Between 1937 and 1945, of the 24 million deaths caused in wars instigated by Japan, 20 million were civilian.

If the Rape of Nanjing cannot properly be termed a genocidal war of annihilation, the massacre nonetheless marked a significant escalation in the violence of the Japanese forces and opened the way for a succession of Japanese mass killings: the "cleansing" of the Chinese communities of Singapore on February 18 and March 3, 1942; the sack of Manila in February 1945; and crimes committed against civilians in Manchuria, the Philippines, and the Dutch East Indies.

In summer 1942, having secured control of territory inhabited by some 500 million people, Japan accelerated its program of plunder and enslavement. The treatment meted out to Japanese prisoners, both Asian and non-

The Japanese air force bombards Nanjing to break Chinese army resistance, 1937.
© Rue des Archives

Japanese troops enter Nanjing, 1937.
© Süddeutsche Zeitung / Rue des Archives

Asian, military and civilian, may be justly compared to the worst features of the Nazi concentration camp regime. Hunger and forced labor, for example, on the vast railway construction project linking Burma and Thailand, killed prisoners by the thousands. Population displacement; death marches; the forced prostitution of thousands of "comfort women" in the Philippines, Korea, China, and Indonesia; the secret medical and biological/chemical warfare experiments undertaken on human subjects by Unit 731 in northeastern China, including vivisection: such crimes are profoundly revealing of the nature of Japanese totalitarianism. ∎

Arrest of a Russian woman, USSR, ca. 1941–44.
© Bundesarchiv

A column of Russian prisoners of war captured in the Crimea, USSR, 1942.
© Rue des Archives/Tal

Atrocities on the Eastern Front

The Decisive Importance of the Eruption of War in the East

Although Poland endured Nazi atrocities from the beginning of the war, for the rest of Europe it was the invasion of the USSR that fundamentally changed the nature of the conflict. The war became at the same time a war of conquest, an ideological war, a civil war (in many countries) rooted in hatred and terror, and a war of racial annihilation.

The overwhelming majority of the massacres committed in Europe by the German army (Wehrmacht, Waffen-SS, and police units), as well as by local forces collaborating with them, took place in the East and the Balkans. The principal targets were the elites of the countries invaded by the Germans, communist political cadres, Soviet prisoners of war, and civilian communities—including, above all, Jews.

The Battle against Partisans and Reprisals

Historians estimate that at least 1 million civilians were killed in Eastern Europe in the course of the Nazi war against national partisan groups, including 340,000 deaths in Byelorussia and 300,000 in Russia. In both these countries, and also in Yogoslavia and Greece, thousands of villages were razed to the ground, put to flame, and looted, and their inhabitants shot, hanged, and burned.

In Byelorussia, a single May 1943 antipartisan operation, code-named "Cottbus," claimed 12,000 victims and razed 200 villages. As part >>>

Soviet prisoners share their meager rations in the Sachsenhausen-Oranienburg concentration camp, Germany, 1944.
© AKG-images

A Soviet prisoner of war dressed in rags, inside the Sachsenhausen-Oranienburg compound.
© AKG-images / Ria Novosti

>>> of this campaign, civilians were used in minefields as human minesweepers; 3,000 lost their lives.

The Fate of Soviet Prisoners of War

By the beginning of 1942, more than 2 million Soviet prisoners of war had been executed or had died from maltreatment. In the course of the war, 60 percent of the 5.7 million Soviet prisoners in German camps would die.

These men were also among the first victims (after a group of Roma/Sinti children at Buchenwald) on whom the Nazis experimented with Zyklon B, at Auschwitz, September 2–5, 1941.

The arrival of peace did not put an end to the ordeal of the Soviet prisoners. Considered by the USSR's Communist authorities as dishonored soldiers or even deserters, many were freed from one prison only to be sent to another, now in their homeland. ■

Citizens clear the main arteries of Leningrad, whose siege caused at least 600,000 civilian deaths. USSR, March 1942.
© Ria Novosti

Massive Bombing

Massive aerial bombardment may be considered a form of civilian massacre. It constituted an essential element of the strategy of "total war." ∎

A family in Mannheim, Germany, leaves their home, devastated by Allied aerial bombing in 1944.
© AKG-images / Ullstein Bild

Nighttime bombing of London, November 1941.
© Rue des Archives / AGIP VB

The bombing of Rome by the U.S. Army
Air Force, July 19, 1943.
© Rue des Archives / AGIP

Total War

The Context

BOMBING OF CIVILIAN TARGETS

In total war, the killing of noncombatants cannot be considered "collateral damage." Rather, it constitutes a strategic option. Civilian populations become targets—vague, anonymous—and their destruction is planned. "Strategic bombing" may even lead to the sacrifice of the civilians of a country's own allies for the sake—at least in theory—of achieving military objectives. France, for example, was struck by 600,000 metric tons of bombs during the war, about one fifth of all the bombs dropped over Europe. French civilian casualties are estimated at 60,000 deaths. In Normandy, which was hit especially hard, entire cities were destroyed, not always with convincing justification.

In the wake of World War I, an international commission of jurists convened to draft the Hague Rules of Air Warfare (1923), whose Article 22 states: "Aerial bombardment for the purpose of terrorizing the civilian population, of destroying or damaging private property not of a military character, or of injuring non-combatants is prohibited"—a principle later reiterated verbatim by the United Nations. However, these rules were not formally adopted by the nations concerned and were systematically violated throughout the war by both the Axis and Allies.

Forced population transfers were another ordeal that total war inflicted on civilians. Between 1939 and 1948, including the effects of redrawn borders, historians estimate that at least 40 million Europeans, including 13 to 14 million ethnic Germans, were forcibly displaced.

IMPORTANT EVENTS

On April 13, 1943, Nazi Germany announces the discovery of mass graves in the Katyn Forest, near Smolensk, where 22,000 members of the Polish officer corps and other members of the Polish intelligentsia are buried. Germany and the USSR blame each other for the crime—feeding their relentless propaganda machines until the very end of the war.

On April 19, 1943, Jewish Resistance fighters led by Mordechai Anieliewicz

> "[O]ur war program for the coming fiscal year will cost 56 billion dollars or, in other words, more than half of the estimated annual national income. That means taxes and bonds and bonds and taxes. . . . In a word, it means an 'all-out' war by individual effort and family effort in a united country. . . . No compromise can end that conflict. There never has been—there never can be—successful compromise between good and evil. Only total victory can reward the champions of tolerance, and decency, and freedom, and faith."
>
> *President Franklin Delano Roosevelt, State of the Union address, January 6, 1942*

launch the Warsaw Ghetto Uprising. Despite being very poorly armed and supplied, the Resistance battles the German forces for two weeks before being crushed. The survivors are executed or deported to the death camps, and what remains of the ghetto is burned down or blown up on May 16, 1943.

In Yugoslavia, communist partisans led by Josip Broz Tito increasingly prevail against the German-supported monarchist Chetnik forces of Draža Mihailović beginning in 1943. Toward the end of the war, the communists also successfully resist a German offensive supported by the Croatian fascist forces known as the Ustaša led by Ante Pavelić. After long hesitation, the Allies decide to support Tito.

THE CAMPS

The common, undifferentiated use of the term *death camps* to refer to Nazi Germany's system of concentration camps is liable to lead to considerable confusion. In fact, the camps to which deportees were sent differed according to their functions. It is important to distinguish among three types of camps:

• Extermination camps, such as Treblinka, Sobibor, and Auschwitz-Birkenau (also called Auschwitz II), where arriving deportees, overwhelmingly Jews, are immediately killed.

• Concentration camps, where prisoners of diverse origins are used for forced labor and systematically dehumanized. The death toll at such camps (Dachau,

Buchenwald, Mauthausen, Ravensbrück) is about 40 percent, but varies widely from camp to camp and depends upon the category of prisoners.

• Mixed camps, more complex in structure, such as Auschwitz I and Majdanek, combined a concentration camp with a death camp.

FRANCE

The Milice is founded on January 30, 1943. This new politico-paramilitary organization collaborates actively with the occupying Germans in its suppression of the Resistance and includes armed units known as the Franc-Garde that operate alongside German forces in battles against the Maquis in 1943 and 1944.

On February 16, 1943, Vichy passes a law creating the Service du Travail Obligatoire (STO: Obligatory Work Service), a program that sends young French male workers born in 1920–22 to Germany as forced laborers in exchange for the return of French prisoners of war. The STO expands the requisition program already passed in September 1942. Many of the *réfractaires*, those who refuse to be drafted under the STO, swell the ranks of the Maquis, which will become the main armed force of the Resistance within France.

Jean Moulin is arrested on June 21, 1943, in Caluire, near Lyon. Moulin is interrogated and tortured by Klaus Barbie, head of the Gestao in Lyon, but reveals nothing. He dies, apparently on July 8, on a Germany-bound train.

Total War

The infliction of massive civilian casualties is one of the fundamental characteristics of total war. The transition to total war is both the culmination of a process that was already evident in World War I and a direct consequence of the globalization of the conflict. President Roosevelt refers to the idea in his State of the Union address of 1942.

For the Axis powers, who had counted on rapid victories, and who find themselves forced to adapt to unexpected circumstances, the headlong rush into total war proves unavoidable. The intensifying war effort and wartime rationing become in effect weapons for uniting, mobilizing, and inflaming their peoples.

This 1944 propaganda poster condemns the destruction caused by Allied bombing, showing the names of French cities in flames: "In 6 months the Anglo-American air force has killed 3,112 French men, women, children; injured 5,228 people; destroyed 25 hospitals, 44 churches, 118 schools, 31,177 houses."
Caen Memorial

An Allied bomb identical to those dropped on the cities of Normandy in 1944.
Caen Memorial

THE MILITARY SITUATION, AUTUMN 1942

The air and sea campaigns bring the first signs that the war is turning in favor of the Allies.

In the Pacific, the American victory at Midway on June 5, 1942, followed by landings at Gaudalcanal and the Solomon Islands on June 7, check the Japanese offensive for the first time.

On the Western Front, advances in submarine detection, the introduction of long-range bombers, and stepped-up production of warships in the U.S. set the stage for Allied victory in the Battle of the Atlantic. On the Eastern Front the Germans fail to take Stalingrad, where the Red Army regains the offensive against the Wehrmacht in November. In North Africa, the Allied victory at El Alamein on October 23 enables General Montgomery to launch a counteroffensive that pushes the Germans and Italians >>>

The Concept of Total War

The processes of total war encompass all aspects of national life, subordinated to the pursuit of war objectives; the entire society is involved in the conflict, and private life loses all autonomy. The opponent, demonized without distinction, becomes nothing more than an array of targets for destruction. In total war, nothing less than total victory is acceptable, with the enemy crushed into unconditional surrender. Negotiation and compromise are by definition ruled out. In this totalitarian vision, war becomes a fight to the death, a "struggle for existence," an ideological war of annihilation, with the characteristics of civil or religious wars. In total war, a country no longer fights merely to

conquer or defend territory, but to impose on others its worldview, in a war without limits.

If total war is undertaken by both sides with equal determination and ferocity, nonetheless there may remain differences between their motives and purposes and the methods and intensity with which governments exploit emotions. In World War II, in Nazi Germany and Imperial Japan the signs of national mania and the glorification of war are most evident: extreme nationalism, fanaticism, brutality, denial of reality, obsession with death (e.g., Japanese kamikaze pilots), and absolute lawlessness. ∎

The War in Europe
Autumn 1942

■ Axis countries and their allies
■ Territories under Axis control
□ Occupied "Free Zone"
■ Allied countries
■ Territories under Allied control
□ Neutral countries
— Limitations of the Third Reich
⋯⋯ Limit of Axis forces in Africa, late October 1942
— The Eastern Front, end of November 1942

German Jews are deported to Latvia. On December 13, 1941, 1,000 Jews are sent to Riga, the Latvian capital, on a train from Bielefeld in northwestern Germany, halfway between Hanover and Dortmund.
© AKG-images

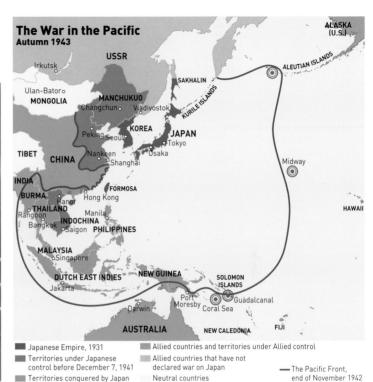

The War in the Pacific
Autumn 1943

■ Japanese Empire, 1931	■ Allied countries and territories under Allied control
■ Territories under Japanese control before December 7, 1941	■ Allied countries that have not declared war on Japan
■ Territories conquered by Japan	■ Neutral countries

— The Pacific Front, end of November 1942

>>> back toward Tunisia. Likewise, Allied troops commanded by General Eisenhower land in Algeria and Morocco to begin Operation Torch on November 8. In response, the Wehrmacht occupies all of France, erasing the boundaries among the various zones of occupation set up in 1940. The Germans invade the Southern Zone (Vichy) on November 11. In response, Vichy scuttles its own fleet in harbor at Toulon on November 27 to prevent its capture by the Reich, while also still refusing to offer its navy to the Allies, in order to preserve France's neutrality according to the terms of the armistice with Germany of June 22, 1940.

Minister of Propaganda Joseph Goebbels gives a speech in the Berlin Sportpalast on June 5, 1943. Built in 1910, the Sportpalast was a multipurpose winter sports venue and meeting hall holding up to 14,000 people. The banner reads "Führer, Command—We Follow!"
© Bundesarchiv

Joseph Goebbels, Reich Minister of Propaganda, 1933–45.
© Bundesarchiv

"In this war there will be neither victors nor vanquished, but only survivors and annihilated."
Joseph Goebbels, speech in the Berlin Sportspalast, January 30, 1943. Translation: R.J. Overy

"I ask you: Do you want total war? If necessary, do you want a war more total and radical than anything that we can even imagine today?"
Hermann Goering, speech in the Berlin Sportspalast, February 18, 1943. Translation: Randall T. Bytwerk

PROPAGANDA
In total war, the weapons of psychological warfare and the manipulation of the masses are indispensable. The control of information and propaganda techniques, which tend to be especially advanced in totalitarian regimes, are decisive in their survival.

"No truce or parley mitigated the strife of the armies. The wounded died between the lines: the dead mouldered into the soil. Merchant ships and neutral ships and hospital ships were sunk on the seas and all on board left to their fate, or killed as they swam. Every effort was made to starve whole nations into submission without regard to age or sex. Cities and monuments were smashed by artillery. Bombs from the air were cast down indiscriminately. Poison gas in many forms stifled or seared the soldiers. Liquid fire was projected upon their bodies. . . . When all was over, Torture and Cannibalism were the only two expedients that the civilized, scientific, Christian States had been able to deny themselves: and they were of doubtful utility."

Winston Churchill, The World Crisis, 1911–1918 *(1923)*

Winston Churchill, prime minister of the United Kingdom, 1940–45.
Caen Memorial

Franklin Delano Roosevelt, president of the U.S., 1933–1945.
© Rue des Archives

Joseph Stalin, general secretary of Central Committee of the Communist Party of the Soviet Union (head of state), 1922–53.
Caen Memorial

NO GOING BACK
By the time Goebbels proclaims the strategy at spectacular rallies in Berlin in January and February 1943, total war has long been a reality, embodied in the logic of rationalized war-industry production, advancing weapons technology, and the continuous increase in the level of violence—which was thought to have reached an unsurpassable level in World War I. Total war signals an irreversible break with the past idea of war as a conflict among states carried out by their armies.

Able-bodied prisoners at the Mauthausen concentration camp were subjected to unspeakable conditions, among which the cruelest was being forced to climb the 186 steps of the camp's quarry, the "Stairs of Death," carrying blocks of stone on their shoulders. Some were forced to jump from the quarry's edge to their deaths.
© AKG-images/Ullstein Bild

A prisoner at Dachau, Germany, 1939.
© AKG-images

The Concentration Camps

Alongside those who the Nazis deported and exterminated because of *what* or *who they were* were those imprisoned for *what they had done*. In Europe, more than 2 million people were deported to concentration camps for acts of resistance, insubordination, or nonconformity. The first inmates of the Third Reich's concentration camps were opponents of the Nazi regime, arrested in 1933. Deportation for the purpose of political repression filled the vast network of camps, where the prisoners' fates varied according to their status, category, and place of internment. Members of the German resistance were especially targeted, and those among them designated NN, for *Nacht und Nebel* (night and fog), disappeared without a trace.

Such prisoners were almost all adults, mostly men, and all assigned to forced labor in the most appalling conditions. Some 800,000 are estimated to have died. Although death was not the main purpose of the concentration camp system as a whole, even prisoners not assigned to "extermination through labor" died from mistreatment, malnutrition, disease, and exhaustion. Inmates were also selected arbitrarily for punishment and execution as part of camp discipline.

Prisoners at the Sachsenhausen-Oranienburg concentration camp, near Berlin, in March 1933.
© FNDIRP

Prisoners during roll call at the Dachau concentration camp, June 28, 1938. Inmates were forced to stand for hours in all weather as a form of punishment.
© Bundesarchiv

Prisoners at the Mauthausen camp in Austria assigned to the construction of a hydroelectric dam. Mauthausen and its vast network of 50 satellite camps were used mainly for the "extermination through labor" of the intelligentisia.
© Association of Former Prisoners at Mauthausen

Prisoners at Sachsenhausen-Oranienburg.
© Bundesarchiv

In France, more than 86,000 people were imprisoned for political reasons, with 85 percent of them originating within France itself. About 60 percent survived. More than 8,800 French women were deported to the Nazi concentration camps, the great majority of them (6,600) to Ravensbrück.

In Germany, certain minorities were persecuted without having committed any crime, and sometimes incarcerated in the concentration camps. This was the case with Jehovah's Witnesses (targeted because they refused to swear allegiance to the Nazi party or serve in the military) and homosexuals. The number of homosexuals interned and killed by the Nazis is difficult to ascertain. In Alsace and the Moselle region, for example, French territory annexed by the Reich, of the approximately 60 arrested for homosexuality, a third were deported to the concentration camps.

The emotional shock that followed the return home of camp inmates after the war led to widespread misunderstanding of the Nazi deportations as a whole. In particular, failure to grasp the diversity of conditions throughout the concentration and extermination camp systems delayed awareness of the scale and uniqueness of the Jewish genocide. ■

**French prisoners of war
return home** under the
Relève program, 1942.
© Keystone France

Mobilization for Total War

The requirements of total war lead
to the development of a closely
integrated network for mobilizing
resources, together with massive
reallocation of labor, mass indoctrination, and control of the tools
of political suppression.

The organization of a war
economy is one of the fundamental requirements of total war. In
Germany, rivalries for power
within the Nazi one-party state
tend to complicate and delay the
process of developing the war
economy. In the U.S. and, to a
lesser degree, the USSR, intensive restructuring of industry enables a rapid conversion to mass
production of war matériel. The
war without question stimulates
research and new inventions on
both sides. However, with a few
important exceptions, the war
effort tends to lead primarily to
the development of ever more
destructive weapons. ∎

The departure of the 100,000th French worker for Germany, presided over by German military authorities, France, November 1941.
© Rue des Archives / Tal

A worker consults the office hours for the bureau in Clermont-Gerrand that places workers in German industry, France, February 1942.
© Keystone France

Workers wait in the Gare de l'Est in Paris for the train that will take them to work in Germany, January 1943.
© Rue des Archives / Tal

The placement office for work in Germany, Paris, 1943.
© Roger Viollet / Bibliothèque Historique de la Ville de Paris
Photo: André Zucca

A Canadian worker assembles magazines for the Bren gun, the primary light machine gun for British and Commonwealth infantry in World War II.
© National Archives of Canada

This American poster celebrates homemakers as part of the war effort, ca. 1941–45.
Caen Memorial

A Canadian poster picturing the union of civilians and soldiers in the war effort, 1943.
Caen Memorial

"European armaments—always more powerful!" A propaganda poster produced in Germany for occupied France glorifying German war industries, ca. 1940–42.
Caen Memorial

A group of U.S. Air Force B-17 bombers photographed during a raid over Germany, ca. 1943–45.
© Bildarchiv Preussicher Kulturbesitz

Bombing Cities

"Strategic bombing" destroys civilian populations anonymously. The flattening of cities by tons of bombs, in defiance of international conventions, signified the crossing of new thresholds of indiscriminate violence in war. The atomic bombs that obliterated Hiroshima and Nagasaki on August 6 and 9, 1945, marked the summit of this escalation.

Ostensibly justified for military reasons, urban aerial bombing, such as the raid on Guernica in 1937, is in reality intended to terrorize civilians. The practice is systematized in 1940 by the German air force with the bombing of Rotterdam (May 14), followed by the raid on Coventry (November 14–15). German air raids on Great Britain result in more than 60,000 casualties.

The Allies rely primarily on the air war in their campaign against Nazi Germany, with the first 1,000-bomber raid, on Cologne, taking place on the night of May 30–31, 1942. Allied bombing of Germany will leave some 600,000 dead and destroy more than 3 million buildings, including many of the country's most important architectural monuments. The RAF alone undertakes 390,000 air raids. The bombings of Hamburg in summer 1943 and of Dresden, on February 13–14, 1945, are among the most lethal. ■

A victim of the German bombing of the Belgian city of Liège, December 17, 1944.
© AKG-images

The Allied bombing of Munich, Germany, 1943.
© Rue des Archives / SVB

A British Ministry of Health poster, 1940.
Caen Memorial

It might be YOU!

CARING FOR EVACUEES IS A NATIONAL SERVICE

ISSUED BY THE MINISTRY OF HEALTH

This German poster, produced in 1941, reads "Blackout" in German, and then, in Polish, "The Enemy Sees Every Light."
© Bundesarchiv

VERDUNKELUNG
wróg widzi każde światło!

The Bund Deutscher Mädel (League of German Girls) learns to use gas masks in a school run by the Luftschutz (Anti-Aircraft Defense), Germany, September 1939.
© AKG-images

A son says good-bye to his mother before joining a partisan unit, USSR, ca. 1941–44.
© Magnum Photos / Mikhail Trakhman

Life in Wartime

The Context

Churchill, Roosevelt, and Stalin meet in Teheran, November 28–December 2, 1943, to discuss military matters. In December 1943 Axis forces respond to Resistance actions with mass executions of hostages in Greece. These reprisals increase the harshness of the brutal suppression that the Greeks have endured since spring 1942. In mid-January 1944, the Soviet army liberates Leningrad, which has been under siege for 900 days, since August 1941.

ASIA

Supported by new aircraft carriers, Fleet Admiral Chester Nimitz, commander in chief of all U.S. and other Allied air, land, and sea forces in the Pacific, proves the effectiveness of a strategy relying on intense bombing by naval aircraft followed by marine invasion in regaining territory lost to the Japanese.

ITALY

Following Allied landings in Sicily, Mussolini is arrested as the Italian government prepares to join the Allies. In September 1943, German troops occupy northern and central Italy and liberate Mussolini, who proclaims the Italian Social Republic (commonly known as the Salò Republic, for the town where Mussolini is headquartered), the second and last Italian fascist state. Hitler forces Il Duce to have five members of the Grand Fascist Council, who had voted against him, including his own son-in-law Count Galeazzo Ciano, shot on January 11, 1944.

FRANCE

Led by General Henri Giraud, commander-in-chief of the Free French Forces (FFL), and in cooperation with the Corsican Resistance, French troops invade the island in early September 1943, defeating the occupying German and Italian garrison by October. This first liberation of a French *département* has powerful symbolic value.

On November 11, the Maquis of the Ain region parade openly through the town of Ononnax, an event covered by the BBC and the underground press.

On January 20, 1944, Vichy passes a law setting up courts martial. These three-judge panels, comprising mostly members of the Milice, pass sentences with no possibility of appeal. Prisoners condemned to death are executed immediately.

Stalin, Rossevelt, and Churchill
at the Teheran conference,
December 1, 1943.
© Rue des Archives

Life in Wartime

It is impossible to generalize about civilian life during World War II. The conflict was too long, and the range of experiences too wide, brutally contrasted, constantly changing, and varied enormously by occupation, ethnicity, and whether the members of a given community lived in an Allied, Axis, or occupied country. All these factors make it equally impossible to characterize any group's collective behavior by a set of simple alternatives or inviolable choices. Nonetheless, in every place touched by the war, despite the privation, suffering, and tragedy, life—leisure, family, romance—went on.

Ration tin of powdered tea with milk and sugar, 1944.
Caen Memorial

British dog tags made from compressed fiber, 1944.
Caen Memorial

TEA RATION 5 ozs.
(containing Tea, Sugar and Soluble Milk Powder)
DIRECTIONS
Use dry spoon and sprinkle powder on the heated water and bring to the boil , stirring until the milk powder is completely dissolved. The contents of the tins are sufficient for 6 pints of tea. For small quantities, 1 oz. (3 heaped teaspoonfuls) are to be added to each pint of water.
TO OPEN TIN INSERT COIN IN CORNER GROOVE AND TURN
SPECIAL NOTE — AFTER FIRST OPENING THIS CAN, REMOVE RUBBER RING FROM THE INSIDE OF THE LID AND BY WRAPPING IT ROUND THE OUTSIDE OF THE CAN AND THE LID, KEEP THE LID RETAINED TIGHTLY TO THE CAN.
REG. DESIGN NO. 714,715 & 809, 365

THE MILITARY SITUATION, SPRING 1943

The spring of 1943 confirms the turning of the tide in favor of the Allies that had begun the previous autumn. On the Eastern Front, the surrender of the 6th Army, led by General Friedrich Paulus, at Stalingrad, on February 2, 1943, has significant repercussions. However, in the short term, its importance is more psychological than strategic, and the Germans retake Kharkov in March.

In North Africa, the Allies, joined by units of the Free French Forces (FFL), control all contested territory after the liberation of Tunisia in May. The Axis no longer has any troops in Africa and loses its strongholds in the western Mediterranean.

On the Western Front, the Battle of the Atlantic turns in favor of the Allies beginning in May 1943. After losing more than 80 submarines, including 41 in May alone, **>>>**

Sabotage of a railway line near Gardanne, France, close to Marseille, ca. 1943–44.
© Bibliothèque de Documentation Internationale Contemporaine (BDIC)-Musée d'Histoire Contemporaine

The Resistance Movements

Life in hiding and armed resistance are the most extreme forms of noncompliance with the occupying fascist regimes: the most heroic, the most dangerous—and the most exceptional. Yet reducing defiance of the occupied solely to the armed struggle distorts our understanding of the complex reality of life under occupation. The story cannot simply be reduced to a clash between resisters and collaborators. Between the two poles of armed resistance and active collaboration lies a wide spectrum of involvement with the occupying government; to see only passivity or complicity represents a vast oversimplification.

Resistance in fact takes many forms that are indirectly related or parallel to the organized Resistance movements and the armed struggle. Subversive discourse, the underground press, inner "spiritual" resistance, rescuing people persecuted by the regime, and aiding those it condemns as outlaws are all forms of what is termed civil or nonviolent resistance.

Unspectacular and usually anonymous, all such gestures confront oppression and constitute humble forms of disobedience and defiance, ordinary acts of resistance in daily life. They convey the reality of nonconsent

The War in Europe
Spring 1943

Axis countries and their allies
Territories under Axis control
— Borders of the Third Reich

Allied countries
Territories under Allied control
Neutral countries

— The Eastern Front, July 1943

to a social and politial order established by force, whether by an occupying power or a despotic state. Even if most such individual acts do not make anyone a resister per se, in the aggregate they bear witness to shared feeling.

In France, for example, the crowds that gather, despite threats from the authorities, for the funerals of shot-down Allied pilots and members of the Resistance executed by the Germans have tremendous symbolic value. The fabric of dissent and silent solidarity is indispensable to the survival and growth of the organized Resistance.

In Italy, in the confusion that follows the signing of the armistice with the Allies, tens of thousands of soldiers suddenly find themselves left to their own devices or desert in order to evade service in the army of the Salò Republic. In many areas, local women take in these men and hide them—an unprecedented spontaneous expression of solidarity. ∎

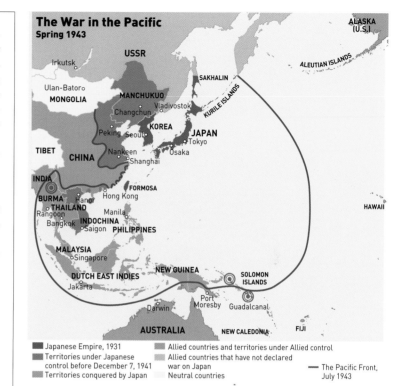

The War in the Pacific
Spring 1943

- ■ Japanese Empire, 1931
- ■ Territories under Japanese control before December 7, 1941
- ■ Territories conquered by Japan
- ■ Allied countries and territories under Allied control
- Allied countries that have not declared war on Japan
- Neutral countries
- — The Pacific Front, July 1943

>>> Grand Admiral Karl Donitz, commander-in-chief of the German navy, puts an end to German submarine attacks on Allied convoys.

In the Pacific, Allied victory at the Battle of Midway brings Japanese expansion to an abrupt halt. After seven months of fierce combat, American and Australian forces succeed in driving the Japanese off Guadalcanal. General Douglas MacArthur and Fleet Admiral Nimitz begin the progressive reconquest of the Pacific islands and other territories invaded by the Japanese.

Members of the Corsican Resistance, 1943.
© DITE

A wartime wedding at the Église de la Madeleine in Paris, ca. 1940–44.
© Bibliothèque de Documentation Internationale Contemporaine (BDIC)–Musée d'Histoire Contemporaine

A French prisoner of war returns home to his wife from prison in Germany in 1945.
© Keystone / Eyedea

War and Private Life

All over the world, forced separations, the struggle for survival, daily life under occupation, and the need for secrecy shattered family life, marriages, and romantic relationships, often with tragic results.

Total war compelled people to sacrifice almost everything for the common cause, erasing all personal concerns. The state interfered constantly in private life, including matters of sexuality, which it attempted to control. Nonetheless, for most ordinary people, romantic relationships remained at the heart of daily life.

War and secrecy encouraged behavior outside socially accepted norms and illicit affairs. Transgression was common, and took diverse forms, including liaisons with occupying soldiers or officials. The consequences of such affairs varied drastically for the two sexes—only women, for example, could get pregnant. ∎

Having Fun in Occupied Paris

Posters advertizing shows in occupied Paris.
© Roger Schall

Sheet music for a Charles Trenet song, "Swing Troubadour," 1941. Trenet was criticized by the Resistance press for performing in cabarets frequented by the occupying Germans.
Caen Memorial

German soldiers enjoy an evening at the Cabaret du Lapin Agile in the Montmartre nightclub district in Paris, ca. 1940–44.
© Roger Schall

Intellectuals, painters, editors, and filmmakers continued to frequent the Café de Flore throughout the Occupation, Paris, ca. 1940–44.
© Rue des Archives

The Palais Garnier opera house, half hidden by German traffic signs, Paris, 1944.
© Keystone / Eyedea

German soldiers sunbathing at the Pont d'Iéna in Paris, ca. 1940–44.
© Sipa Press

Battle rages in the streets of Leningrad, former home of the Czars, October 1942.
© Magnum / Yakov Ryumkin

Life and Death of a Soldier

The soldier's life has been described in many ways, as has his dilemma in the face of death: that he must kill in order not to be killed. Some soldiers speak of death in battle as the ultimate sacrifice. Some emphasize their hatred of war; others confess their fascination with armed violence and the logic of war, and even admit to taking pleasure in slaughter. During World War II, the development of total war drove the troops' capacity both for self-sacrifice and endurance of suffering, as well as for the worst barbarity, beyond previous limits. No army emerged unscathed, but otherwise the extreme diversity of the soldiers' experiences precludes any generalizations. For example, some were executed as prisoners of war; some were part of units deliberately sacrificed by their commanding officers; some

A glass bottle found near a soldier's body without dog tags. The name of the soldier (Grenadier Otto Fischer of the 6th SS Mountain Division "Nord") was written on the slip of paper inside.
Collection of the Deutsche Dienststelle (WASt), Berlin

A U.S. marine comforts a gravely wounded comrade during the invasion of the island of Okinawa, Japan, April 1942.
© Magnum / W. Eugene Smith

British, Commonwealth, and American soldiers land not far from Salerno, near Naples, September 8, 1943. In the foreground, British soldiers.
© Imperial War Museum

participated in mass slaughter of defenseless civilians. Nonetheless, an excessively relativistic view is not justified: the Allies fought for a vision of the world directly opposed to the one that the Axis powers sought to impose by force. Methodical indoctrination in Nazi and Imperial Japanese ideologies schooled entire nations in fanatical violence, corrupting the heroic ideal of the warrior and making unprecedented carnage merely commonplace. ■

Celebrating VE Day in London, May 8, 1945.
© DITE / USIS

Reconquest and Liberation

ITALY

After the failure of his attempt to negotiate with the Italian Resistance, Mussolini is arrested by partisans on April 28, 1945, while attempting to flee to Germany together with the ministers of the Saló Republic and other fascist officials. He and his mistress, Carla Petacci, are summarily executed. Their bodies are taken to Milan and hung upside down in the Piazzale Loreto, where, the year before, the Germans and Italian Fascists had shot fifteen Milanese civilians in retaliation against partisan activity.

GREECE

After the departure of the Germans and the liberation of Athens in October 1944, violent clashes erupt between the two main groups of the Resistance, the communist EAM-ELAS (the National Liberation Front and its military wing) and the right-wing monarchist EDES (National Republican Greek League). An armistice imposed in January 1945 by British forces does not bring peace. Brutal purges of suspected collaborators by ELAS is followed by a "white terror" in which right-wing reprisals leave thousands dead. Greece explodes into all-out civil war, which will tear the country apart from 1946 to 1949.

POLAND

The Red Army liberates the last remaining inmates of Auschwitz on January 27, 1945. The SS has already blown up the gas chambers and crematoria at Birkenau to hide German atrocities from the advancing Soviet troops and evacuated the camp a few days before.

GERMANY

On July 20, 1944, Colonel Claus von Stauffenberg, leader of a conspiracy within the Wehrmacht officer corps, attempts to assassinate Hitler with a bomb during a high-level briefing. Although the bomb causes four deaths and many injuries, Hitler escapes barely wounded. Hitler responds with a ruthless purge that continues to the war's last days, with nearly 5,000 executed and many forced to commit suicide,

Four women accused of collaborating with the Germans are displayed in public after having their hair shaved or hacked off on August 26, 1944, in the town of Montereau-Fault-Yonne (about 40 miles southeast of Paris), shortly after liberation by American forces. © DITE / USIS

including Field Marshal Rommel. The military hierarchy is in effect decapitated, and the organized resistance movement within Germany destroyed. Hiding in his bunker below the Reich Chancellery in Berlin with his closest associates, Hitler commits suicide on April 30, 1945, together with his mistress Eva Braun, whom he had married two days before. Minister of Propaganda Joseph Goebbels does likewise, taking his family into death with him.

THE U.S.

At age 62, FDR is re-elected by a wide majority to a fourth term on November 7, 1944. He dies suddenly on April 12, 1945, from a cerebral hemorrhage, less than a month before the Allied victory over Nazi Germany. Vice President Harry S. Truman succeeds FDR as president.

JAPAN

On August 6, 1945, at 8:15 a.m., the B-29 bomber Enola Gay drops the world's first atomic bomb on the city of Hiroshima. Three days later, a second bomb destroys Nagasaki. An estimated 250,000 are killed, not including the tens of millions of survivors doomed to die shortly of radiation poisoning.

President Truman's decision to use the bomb is intended to end the war immediately, avoiding the heavy losses of both American forces and Japanese civilians that would have followed an invasion of Japan. Reactions range from enthusiastic approval to anxious doubt. Almost alone in his protest, the French novelist Albert Camus writes on August 8, in an editorial in the newspaper Combat, "Mechanized civilization has just reached the ultimate stage of savagery."

FRANCE

General de Gaulle returns to France on June 14, 1944, almost four years to the day after having left for London. In order to assert the authority of his exiled Provisional Government of the French Republic, which is not considered legitimate by President Roosevelt, de Gaulle appoints François Coulet Commissioner of the Republic for Normandy. Coulet in turn replaces the Vichy sub-prefect in Bayeux with his own assistant, Raymond Triboulet. The Provisional Government, with de Gaulle as president, is recognized on October 23, 1944, by the U.S.

The shaving of women accused of collaboration or of having intimate relationships with the occupying Germans has become a familiar image of the purges that followed the liberation of France. Accused in haste and often wrongly, about 20,000 women have their heads shaved.

Reconquest and Liberation

In the Pacific and in Asia, as in North Africa previously, the balance of power tilts in the Allies' favor in 1943. Likewise, on every European front where decisive battles are fought, the Axis forces lose ground. Despite their uneven pace of retreat and some temporary Allied setbacks, the tide has turned irreversibly. The victorious Allied advance ends with the unconditional surrender of Nazi Germany on May 8, 1945.

In the Far East and in Southeast Asia, the Allies' methodical reconquest of territory from the Japanese encounters the stiff resistance of the fanatically determined Imperial Army, which leads the U.S. to drop two atomic bombs on Japan, thus ending the conflict in August 1945.

With their countless battles, massive urban bombing, eruptions of civil war, and indiscriminate reprisals against entire communities, the wars of liberation complete the devastation of Europe and Asia. Both continents end the ordeal exhausted. With the exception of Great Britain, most of the European countries involved in the war lie in ruins, and all are shaken by the discovery of the horrors perpetrated by the Nazis; some remain profoundly divided at the end of hostilities and face an uncertain fate.

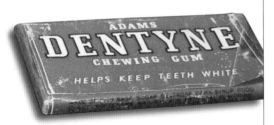

American chewing gum, a novelty that U.S. soldiers sometimes shared with civilians they met in Europe, ca. 1944.
Caen Memorial

THE MILITARY SITUATION, AUTUMN 1943–EARLY 1944
Beginning in autumn 1943, after a series of ever more obvious signs of weakening, Germany suffers a series of setbacks.

The Eastern Front
After Stalingrad, and despite a brief German counterattack in spring 1943, the Red Army regains the offensive commandingly. By spring 1944, all Soviet territory has been liberated.

The Western Front
The arrival of American, British, and Commonwealth forces in Sicily in July 1943, followed by the fall of Mussolini and a second landing at the southern end of the Italian peninsula in September, reverse Axis prospects in Italy. With the support of king Victor Emmanuel III, Marshal Pietro Badoglio is appointed prime minister, **>>>**

Resistance

In Europe, except in the USSR and the Balkans, the armed Resistance never had any decisive effect as a military force on the general course of the war. On the other hand, it did play a determining role in certain circumstances, especially during the Liberation phase.

In France, for example, the Resistance was effective in providing the Allies with intelligence, in acts of sabotage, and in guerilla tactics that slowed down, put pressure on, or delayed the occupying troops, all of which contributed to the success of the Allied landings of June 6, 1944 (D-Day) and August 14 (the corresponding landings in the South of France).

Beyond its military impact, it was above all the Resistance, both inside and outside France, that helped erase the feeling of national humiliation lingering from the German invasion of June 1940, and which enabled France to avoid the further humiliation of finding itself governed by foreign armies after the end of the war. With its honor at least partly restored, France was able to take its place beside the victorious Allies when Nazi Germany surrendered.

The Resistance in all its diverse forms remained above all a moral revolt. For the future, its most significant legacy is without doubt the invaluable testimony of those who resisted: accounts of their experiences, the evidence they leave for historians, their bearing witness.

The Maquis of the Vercors, Summer 1944
The killing of the Maquis in the Vercors region, a high plateau in southeastern France, is one of the best-known episodes in the whole tragic history of the Resistance during the battles immediately preceding Liberation. In June 1944, 4,000 Maquisards gathered there in the euphoric atmosphere that followed the proclamation of the short-lived Free Republic of the Vercors, impatiently awaiting expected Allied parachute drops of armaments. The German attack began on July 21 with 10,000 men, exceptionally well supplied and reinforced by paratroop units. The Maquis were routed and scattered in only three days, **>>>**

The War in Europe
Autumn 1943–early 1944

Axis countries and their allies
Territories under Axis control
Italy under German occupation
Allied countries
Territories under Allied control
Neutral countries
— Borders of the Third Reich
— The Eastern Front, spring 1944

>>> which were followed by nearly a week of horrific reprisals against the Maquis fighters, including the wounded, and local civilians. The death toll was heavy: 456 victims, including 130 civilians.

After the war, the massacre of the Vercors became the subject of intense polemical dispute regarding the consequences of the Maquisards' vainly waiting for reinforcements and help from the Free French organization based in London, even as the area became one of the most honored memorial sites of the Resistance. The tragedy of the Vercors exemplifies characteristics of the Resistance: the defiant affirmation of liberty, the involvement of young people, the diverse origins and political affiliations of the fighters, the misunderstandings and miscommunication between the Resistance inside and outside France, the Maquisards' sometimes vague tactics, the secondary place of the Resistance in Allied plans, the heroism of the fighters, and the martyrdom of local communities. ■

The War in the Pacific
Autumn 1943–early 1944

Japanese Empire, 1931
Territories under Japanese control before December 7, 1941
Territories conquered by Japan
Allied countries and territories under Allied control
Allied countries that have not declared war on Japan
Neutral countries
— The Pacific Front, autumn 1943

Weapons and other matériel are parachuted in broad daylight by the Allies into the Vercors region in southeastern France, June 25, 1944.
© Imperial War Museum

>>> signs an armistice with the Allies, and declares war on Germany, which immediately invades, occupying northern and central Italy. The Allied advance up the peninsula is blocked in the Apennine mountains until spring 1944.

In the Pacific
Starting in autumn 1943, with the aid of forces from Australia and New Zealand and under the command of General MacArthur and Admiral Nimitz, the Americans take control of the Solomon Islands and retake the Gilbert and Marshall Islands, which represent the eastern limits of Japanese conquest. The Allies definitively confirm their superiority in the air and at sea.

Mourners at the funerals of children killed in the confrontation with German troops during the uprising in Naples, Italy, October 2, 1943.

Reprisals in Western Europe

Familiar images of the German army contrast the savagery of its war of annihilation in the East with its "correct" conduct in the war and occupation of the West. Considering the number of victims, the day-to-day treatment of entire communities and their fates at German hands, there is indeed simply no comparison to be made between Western and Eastern Europe.

However considerable the differences among the Germans' uses of violence in the various theaters of the war, it is important not to diminish the extreme harshness of their political repression in Western Europe, beginning in winter 1943–44. Justified in German eyes by the struggle against the "terrorists" of the Resistance, the occupiers' reprisals take the same extreme forms as they do on the Eastern Front. Their main victims are always civilians, including women and children.

In Belgium, Italy, and France, alongside the deportations, the Germans take various measures that increasingly create a climate of terror. Most notable on a long list of massacres are those at Stavelot, near Bastogne, Belgium; the Fosse Ardeatine in Rome and the village of Marzabotto, Italy; and in France the "Bloody Easter" in the Jura mountains, and the killings at Villeneuve d'Ascq, Tulle, Oradour-sur-Glane, Saint-Genis-Laval, Maillé, and Vassieux-en-Vercors—among many others. ■

Women of the village of Kertch, in the Crimea, searching for family members among those executed by the Germans. USSR, January 1942.
© Magnum / Dimitri Baltermants

The village of Oradour-sur-Glane, France, after the massacre perpetrated by the 2nd Armored Division of the Waffen-SS "Das Reich" in June 1944.
© ECPAD

Civilians hanged by the SS in an unidentified city.
© Bibliothèque de Documentation Internationale Contemporaine (BDIC)–Musée d'Histoire Contemporaine

A party of French partisan snipers, members of a communist Resistance group, arrested by the Milice in the Northern Zone, is reviewed by members of a Wehrmacht Propaganda Company (who shot the photo) in 1944.
© Bundesarchiv

One of the photos of a 1944 hanging in France, discovered in an SS officer's briefcase in May 1945.
© Bibliothèque de Documentation Internationale Contemporaine (BDIC)–Musée d'Histoire Contemporaine

France in 1944

Though circumstances vary considerably from place to place in France in 1944, several factors converge to make daily life unbearable for millions. Intensified Allied bombing, especially of Normandy and the Breton coast, kills or injures tens of thousands. At the same time, the French-on-French violence of the *guerre franco-française* claims numerous victims as the Resistance clashes with collaborators, prompting more aggressive reprisals by the Milice. Finally, German units, doubly threatened by Resistance "terrorists" and the prospect of defeat, unleash ever more indiscriminate assaults on civilians—the mur-derous swath cut through the southwest and the Massif Central by the 2nd Armored Division of the Waffen-SS nicknamed "Das Reich" provides one infamous example. The disorder and explosions of violence that in some places accompany Liberation tend to be in proportion to the suffering that precedes it.

The Purges
In Europe as a whole, several million people have supported, to varying degrees, the cause of Nazi Germany. In the occupied countries, the liberation of their lands is not sufficient to close the book on the war for many. Public opinion demands the punishment **>>>**

This German army propaganda photo shows the arrest of a communist member of the French Resistance in July 1944. French Resistance cells tended to organize themselves along the lines of political groupings that preceded the Occupation.
© Bundesarchiv

A note addressed to the commandant of the Feldgendarmerie, the German military police, betraying three members of the Resistance to the Nazi authorities.

>>> of collaborators everywhere. Resistance organizations insist upon it as necessary for healing the rifts of the war years. Justice is demanded not only for moral reasons, and out of a desire to keep faith with the dead, but because reconstruction, even the very possibility of the future, depends upon it.

Termed *épuration*—purification, purging, cleansing—in France, the punishment of collaborators takes different forms depending on local culture, history, and each nation's judgment of collaborators' actions and behavior. In some cases, entire groups are punished (for example, Soviet prisoners of war); in others, collaborators are confronted by popular tribunals, summary executions, lynchings, mass killings (as in Yugoslavia), or the reintroduction of the death penalty (in the Scandinavian countries). In France, the judicial process of *épuration* involves a considerable range in the severity of punishments meted out, which vary by time, place, and jurisdiction. French courts consider the cases of more than 300,000 accused collaborators. Of these, 125,000 go to trial: three-quarters are found guilty, with 44,000 sentenced to prison. Special courts, *chambers civiques*, are convened to hear cases of "national indignity" and condemn 50,000 French citizens to "national degradation." Extrajudicial *épuration*—in effect, lynch mobs and vigilantes—claim 9,000 to 10,000 lives, almost all between June 6, 1944, and the restoration of the French judicial system. Of the 7,055 death sentences passed lawfully by civil and military tribunals, 1,700 are carried out.

Épuration leaves France divided. Public criticism allows for the airing of legitimate opinions for and against. Some controversies, such as the bitter dispute between the writers Albert Camus (who favored punishment of all collaborators) and François Mauriac (who advocated national reconciliation) do elevate the debate. ■

French women arrested by the Milice, probably for their links to the Resistance, Brittany, July 16, 1944.
© Eyedea / Keystone

Athenians celebrate the return of the Greek government led by Georgios Papandreou from exile, October 18, 1944.
© Imperial War Museum

Liberation

In Europe, more than the day of Germany's official surrender, it is the prior moment of Liberation that everywhere marks the real end of the war throughout Europe. This period varies from country to country, and from region to region within each country, and lasts from a few days to several weeks.

From Kiev (November 6, 1943) to La Rochelle and Lorient (May 9, 1945), the Liberation period lasts nearly a year and a half. Rome is not liberated until June 4, 1944; Brussels on September 7; Athens on October 12; Auschwitz-Birkenau and Warsaw in January 1945; Vienna in mid-April.

Both with and without the inter-vention of Allied forces, the major-ity of French territory is liberated in August and September 1944. Like the multitude that welcomes de Gaulle to Paris on August 26, 1944, the crowds exploding with joy that accompany the restoration of freedom express the emotions of a country reunited around the Resistance and La France Libre, de Gaulle's restored free French government. In an atmosphere of festivity mixed with mourning, and despite some instances of popular violence that express a more or less spontaneous desire for revenge, France strives to re-store national harmony through-out a summer without equal in the nation's history. ■

More than 200 French female political prisoners, condemned to death by the Germans, are liberated by American infantry in Hagenau, Alsace, on December 11, 1944.
© DITE / USIS

British and American servicemen celebrate VE Day with civilians in London, May 8, 1945.
© DITE / USIS

French children greet the arrival of American troops in Barfleur, Normandy, in June 1944.
© DITE / USIS

French civilians rejoice following the surrender of the last pocket of German resistance in the port town of Saint-Nazaire, on the Atlantic coast, on May 11, 1945.
© DITE / USIS

THE MILITARY SITUATION, SUMMER 1944–SUMMER 1945

The Western Front

In Italy, the Allied forces break through in the Apennines at Monte Cassino in May 1944 and liberate Rome by the beginning of June. Against a background of civilian reprisals and civil war in the North, Italy will not be entirely liberated until spring 1945, with the collapse of the Gothic Line established by the Germans south of the Po River valley in central Italy.

In France, long and violent battles follow the Allied landings on June 6 in Normandy. The German lines are breached in August; Paris is liberated on August 25; and Allied landings in Provence, in southern France on August 15, are followed by the general retreat of the occupying forces, harassed by the Resistance. The Wehrmacht however succeeds in regrouping its forces as they approach German territory. After defeating the last major German counteroffensive in the Ardennes forest in Belgium and northern France in the Battle of the Bulge, in December 1944–January 1945, the Allies cross the Rhine in March, all the while deluging Germany with aerial bombardment. American forces meet the Red Army at Torgau on the River Elbe on April 25, 1945.

The Eastern Front

Once Soviet territory is liberated, in spring 1944, Soviet forces successively occupy Romania, Bulgaria, Finland, and part of Hungary, all former German allies. In Yugoslavia, Tito's partisans overthrow the occupying German regime. The Poles attempt to drive the Germans out on their own, but the Warsaw Uprising is mercilessly suppressed by the Germans, while the >>>

The War in Europe
Summer 1944–Summer 1945

Axis countries and their allies
Territories under Axis control
Axis countries joining the Allies

Allied countries
Territories under Allied control
Neutral countries

— Borders of the Third Reich
···· The Fronts before Operation Bragation, summer 1944
— The Fronts, end of 1944

A column of Soviet tanks rolls along a heavily bombed street in Berlin, April 1945.
© AKG-images

On Elbe Day, April 25, 1945, U.S. and Soviet forces meet for the first time on German soil when a patrol from an intelligence and reconnaissance platoon of the 69th Infantry Division of the U.S. 1st Army meets forward elements of the Soviet 58th Guards Division, a rifle regiment of the Soviet 5th Guards Army, near Strehla, Germany. Here, the next day, for photographers, the U.S. and Soviet soldiers shake hands on a ruined bridge over the River Elbe, near Torgau in Saxony.

>>> Red Army, drawn up outside the city, declines to intervene, content to see the Poles slaughtered once more. The city is liberated on January 17. At the end of winter 1944–45, the Soviets cross the Oder River, enter Prague and Vienna, and encircle Berlin, which they take on May 2, 1945. Two days earlier, on April 30, Hitler commits suicide.

The Pacific and the Far East

The American navy, marines, and naval air force continue the reconquest of territory invaded by Japan, putting Japan itself within reach of the B-29 Flying Fortress bombers. Tokyo is bombed in November 1944. After driving the Japanese from New Guinea, General MacArthur launches the Philippines campaign in October 1944.

Beginning in 1945, freed by the imminent defeat of Germany in Europe, the Allied forces (the USSR excepted) launch a widespread offensive against Japan, including Burma, China, and Indonesia. After the Allied victory at Iwo Jima in March 1945, the occupation of Okinawa in June enables nearly uninterrupted U.S. air raids against Japanese cities.

The atomic bombs dropped on Hiroshima and Nagasaki on August 6 and 9 leave Japan no choice but unconditional surrender, which is concluded on August 14.

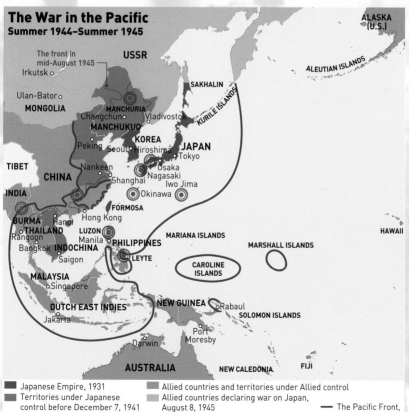

The War in the Pacific
Summer 1944–Summer 1945

- Japanese Empire, 1931
- Territories under Japanese control before December 7, 1941
- Territories conquered by Japan
- Allied countries and territories under Allied control
- Allied countries declaring war on Japan, August 8, 1945
- Neutral countries
- The Pacific Front, end of 1944

Unidentified bodies recovered from the rubble after the destruction of Dresden, Germany, by Allied firebombing are piled in a heap to be burned, February 1945.
© Bundesarchiv

Costs and Consequences: Emerging from Wartime

In 1968 the United Nations General Assembly adopted a draft convention declaring war crimes and crimes against humanity beyond all national statutory limitations, providing a legal basis for the prosecution of perpetrators of genocide. In France, where such a law had already been passed on December 26, 1964, charges were consequently brought against Klaus Barbie, Paul Touvier, René Bousquet, and Maurice Papon.

Deportation, the technology of the gas chambers, and the sheer scale of the massacres, all made the crimes of World War II seem distant, impersonal, invisible. Mass murder had transformed its human victims into abstract targets and diluted individual responsibility for their deaths.

The atomic bombing of Nagasaki, August 9, 1945.
© DITE

SATURATION BOMBING AND ATOMIC WEAPONS

During the trials at Nuremberg and in Tokyo, the question of the Allies' massive bombing campaigns against civilian targets was not raised. Beyond the number of deaths involved, including the death toll in friendly countries, it is fair to question the reasoning behind the intensification of Allied bombing in the final months of the war.

The atomic bombs dropped on Hiroshima and Nagasaki have elicited conflicting judgments on their meaning and implications. While some saw in the bomb a weapon of deterrence and a radical means of halting potential aggressor nations, others proposed that the recourse to nuclear weapons signified an acceptance of the inevitable end of the human race.

CHINA

In China, despite the façade of a peace agreement in October 1945, clashes multiply between the communist forces let by Mao Zedong and those of the Guomindang under Chiang Kai-shek, who is supported by the U.S. Civil war erupts anew in the summer of 1946.

GERMANY

No peace treaties are signed with Germany after the war. Rather, its fate is decided in a series of conferences among the three major Allied powers, the U.S., the USSR, and Great Britain. Germany is forced to surrender a considerable part of its territory in the east. Counting those who fled the advance of the Red Army and those expelled from territory recaptured or annexed by the USSR, Poland, and Czechoslovakia, an estimated 13 to 14 million ethnic Germans are displaced.

THE RETURN OF PRISONERS OF WAR

Soldiers were taken prisoner during World War II in unprecedented numbers. In Europe alone, the Allies detained 11 million in 1945, and 9 million were held by the Germans in the course of the war.

Of the 1.8 million French soldiers captured in 1940, nearly 1 million are still in captivity when hostilities end. Combined with the return of French deportees who have survived the camps and men conscripted for forced labor through the Obligatory Work Service program, the soldiers' repatriation extends over several months, often spent in difficult conditions. The bitterness they feel at their sometimes less-than-warm welcome home is exacerbated by their inability to comprehend the problems and changes that have arisen in the country they left five years before.

Although posters issued by the government exhort the public to equal treatment of the three groups of returnees—"They are united; don't divide them"—prisoners of war cannot help being aware of their place in national memory. They discover that they represent a defeat that must be forgotten and, at the same time, that their sufferings, however painful, cannot be compared to the tragic fate of those deported to the concentration and death camps. The returning deportees, moreover, are perceived *en bloc*, as undifferentiated victims, and met with stunned incredulity.

POSTWAR TRIALS IN FRANCE

After surrendering to the authorities on April 24, 1945, Marshal Pétain is tried before the High Court from July 23 to August 15. Silent throughout his long trial, he is condemned to death by majority vote of the tribunal. However, the court expresses a further wish that the sentence should not be carried out. Pardoned by de Gaulle, his sentence commuted to life in prison, Pétain will end his days on the Île d'Yeu, off the French Atlantic coast, dying on July 23, 1951, at the age of 95.

Costs and Consequences: Emerging from Wartime

A poster exhorting merchants to accept as legal tender the *bons de retour,* vouchers issued to returning prisoners of war and deportees, France, ca. 1945–46
Caen Memorial

Badge issued to men who had been conscripted for forced labor in Germany through the STO (Obligatory Work Service) program, for their return to France in 1945.
Caen Memorial

Total war on a global scale has shattered the established international order. The bloodiest mass slaughter in history, a massacre of unimaginable proportions, has left humanity traumatized the world over. In response, the Allies resolve to try high officials of the Axis countries before an international military tribunal, and to enshrine in international law the concepts of war crimes and crimes against humanity.

Europe, which has been for six years one vast battlefield, the scene of countless tragedies, and the site of the absolute evil symbolized by Auschwitz, has lost status, power, and influence. The U.S. and the USSR are the great victors in the conflict, but their alliance cannot long resist their conflicting national interests and the antagonism fed by their opposing ideologies. At the same time, the European colonies and the so-called underdeveloped nations of the Third World, many of whom have contributed to the Allied victory, rise up to demand freedom and economic justice.

The lack of political realism in the aftermath of World War I doomed the League of Nations and led only to another war; now, the renewed will to build a new world order that will lay the groundwork for a durable peace results in the founding of the United Nations. In Western Europe, awareness of the continent's decline and of the suicidal consequences of the divisions that have torn it apart revives the project of European union.

CHANGING BORDERS: EUROPE IN 1945

In Central and Eastern Europe, the map is drastically redrawn by the ambition and the power of the Soviet Union. The USSR expands westward with the annexation of new territories, including the Baltic states, the northern part of East Prussia (including the city of Königsberg), eastern Poland, Bessarabia, and the eastern parts of Czechoslovakia. In compensation for the lands lost to the USSR, Poland's western border is shifted 125 miles westward to the Oder and Neisse Rivers, annexing Pomerania, Silesia, and the southern part of East Prussia. The Red Army occupies Poland, Czechoslovakia, Hungary, Romania, Bulgaria, >>>

The Death Toll

A precise tally of the human losses during World War II is impossible for many reasons: the enormous destructive force unleashed on several continents, massacres that remain unknown, the inclusion in the tally of civilian victims of military personnel whose status is often poorly defined. Approximate estimates range from 50 to 60 million deaths.

Military losses, civilian losses

Civilian losses are at least equal to and almost certainly surpass military losses, with 30 million civilian deaths out of an estimated worldwide total of 55 million, and ratios that vary drastically from country to country.

The war in the Pacific is thought to have caused 20 to 25 million deaths in Asia, or about 40 percent of the worldwide total, three-quarters of them civilians.

In some countries, military losses outnumber civilian losses:

- in the USSR, with 13.5 million military dead out of a total of 21 million, or 65%;
- in Germany, with 4 out of 7 million total, or 57%;
- in Japan, with 2.7 out of 3 million, or 90%;
- in Great Britain, with 340,000 out of 400,000, or 85%;
- in the U.S., with 300,000 military deaths, or 100% of the total.

In other countries, civilian losses outnumber military losses:

- in China, where estimates range from 14.5 to 20 million civilian deaths, about 75% of the total;

Europe in 1945

Allied countries
Axis countries that joined the Allies during the war
U.S. sphere of influence

USSR and annexed territories
Soviet sphere of influence
Neutral countries

Occupied zones
Borders within occupied sectors
City under four-power occupation (USA, USSR, U.K., and France)

Former borders
The fronts on May 8, 1945

- in Poland, with 5.3 million, or 95% of the total;
- in Yugoslavia, with 1.4 million, or 75%.
- in France, with 0.3 million out of 0.5 million dead, or 60% of the total.

Research that aims to verify the exact numbers of casualties in the war and the proportion of civilian to military losses has its place, but the results remain uncertain, and of doubtful utility. On such a scale, precise statistics can only be moderately helpful in conveying the horrifying reality of the facts involved. ■

ABOVE: **Bodies of 67 Resistance fighters shot by the Germans** are exhumed from a mass grave and prepared for reburial, Beauvilliers, Burgundy, December 9, 1944.
© ECPAD

LEFT (BACKGROUND): **A mass grave of civilian victims of Allied bombing,** near Paris, 1943.
© Eyedea / Keystone

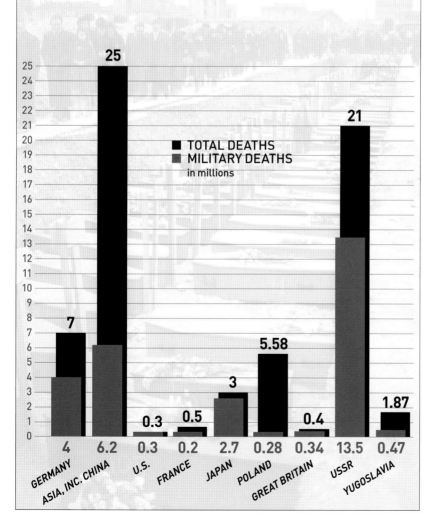

TOTAL DEATHS
MILITARY DEATHS
in millions

	GERMANY	ASIA, INC. CHINA	U.S.	FRANCE	JAPAN	POLAND	GREAT BRITAIN	USSR	YUGOSLAVIA
Total deaths	7	25	0.3	0.5	3	5.58	0.4	21	1.87
Military deaths	4	6.2	0.3	0.2	2.7	0.28	0.34	13.5	0.47

>>> Albania, and Yugoslavia, as well as part of Austria and Germany. Having lost part of its eastern territory, Germany is divided into four zones of occupation controlled respectively by the U.S., USSR, Great Britain, and France. Berlin, which lies in the Soviet zone, is also divided into corresponding quadrants. In Austria, Vienna is likewise divided. Italy loses its possessions on the Adriatic coast (Istria and Trieste) to Yugoslavia (though in 1954, Trieste will be returned to Italian control). Minor adjustments are also made to the border between Italy and France.

The city of Caen, in Normandy, after the Allied bombing of 1944.
Caen Memorial

Moral Shock

The strategies of terror that come increasingly to the fore as the war progresses, the discovery of one mass grave after another, confusion and distress in the face of vast suffering, the incomprehensible monstrousness of the concentration and death camps, and the growing horror attending increasing awareness of the Nazi genocides: all explain the extremity, depth, and long-lasting effects of the moral shock provoked by the war.

If the intensity of the partisan struggles to realize a world opposed to the Nazis and the widespread demographic rebound following the war express an un-conquerable human will to live, the trauma of total war leaves less perceptible but longer-lasting traces.

The Nazi industrialization of death and fears of a nuclear apocalypse leave the hope of continual progress through science badly tarnished. The war years have taught people how to live surrounded daily by indiscriminate violence, torture, racial hatred, inhumanity, and lawlessness of all kinds. The very worst no longer comes as a surprise. Among the tragic heritage of World War II is the discovery of the banality of evil. ∎

Former inmates of Nazi camps during a march organized by the French Communist Party on May 1, 1945. Their banner reads "Political deportees from the camps at Auschwitz-Ravensbrück-Mauthausen: camps of extermination or slow death."
© Rue des Archives

"[A]n iron curtain is drawn down upon their front. We do not know what is going on behind."
Telegram from Winston Churchill to Harry Truman, May 12, 1945

The Summit Meetings

Three summit meetings brought together the three Allied heads of state and laid the foundations for the future world system.

The first took place November 28–December 2, 1943, in Teheran, the capital of Iran, where Churchill, Roosevelt, and Stalin met for the first time face-to-face. This summit was essentially devoted to strategic problems, including the decision to land Allied forces in the West, but it also formulated the broad principles that would underlie the founding of the United Nations at the conference in San Francisco two years later, April 25–June 25, 1945.

A second summit, which took place at Yalta, in the Crimea, February 4–11, 1945, is considered the most important of the three. There, the three leaders decided the fate of Europe, and most notably the fate of Germany and Poland. Contrary to what is often asserted, the division of Europe into two blocs was not determined at Yalta. It resulted, rather, from the failure to honor in Eastern Europe reciprocal commitments made among the three powers to hold elections in all liberated countries. It was shortly after Yalta, and at Churchill's insistence, that France was recognized as one of the occupying powers in Germany.

Stalin was the only one of the three heads of state to attend all three summit meetings. At the final summit, in Potsdam, July 17–August 2, 1945, Harry Truman succeeded Roosevelt, and Clement Attlee, the new British prime minister, replaced Churchill partway through the meeting. While certain provisions of the Potsdam Accords, such as the prosecution of Nazi war crimes, demanded the founding of an effectively functioning international justice system, the negotiations that led to the redrawing of Europe's borders revealed tensions what would rapidly grow worse. ∎

Churchill, Roosevelt (seated), and Stalin at the Yalta conference, February 4–11, 1945.
© Imperial War Museum

International Justice: Genocide and Crimes Against Humanity

war; or persecutions on political, racial or religious grounds."

The original definition was further refined by the 1968 international convention that voided all national statutes of limitations on crimes against humanity. The revised convention also expanded the list of offenses covered, including in particular the "crime of genocide."

Crimes against humanity are, crucially, defined not by the gravity of the alleged offenses, but by the evident intention to contribute to the destruction of a human community because of its identity "on political, racial or religious grounds." ■

Honoring intentions previously affirmed at the Teheran and Yalta summits, the Allies decided on July 26, 1945, during the Potsdam Conference, to create an international military tribunal. The Charter of the Nuremberg Tribunal was drawn up shortly thereafter, and it is in the tribunal's constitution that the notion of crimes against humanity appears for the first time, in article 6(c), which defines such crimes to include "murder, extermination, enslavement, deportation, and other inhumane acts committed against any civilian population, before or during the

ABOVE: *Nazi Atrocities*, **a brochure** produced by the National Front, a French Resistance organization founded in 1941 by the Communist Party.
Caen Memorial

A brochure comprising eyewitness accounts of political prisoners deported to Germany, documents, and photographs assembled by the newspaper *Libération*, June 1945.
Caen Memorial

French prisoners liberated from the Nazi camps arrive at Le Bourget Airport, near Paris, 1945.
© Rue des Archives

HERMANN GOERING
CONDAMNE A MORT

WILHELM KEITEL
CONDAMNE A MORT

ALFRED JODL
CONDAMNE A MORT

JOACHIM
VON RIBBENTROP
CONDAMNE A MORT

JULIUS STREICHER
CONDAMNE A MORT

WILHELM FRICK
CONDAMNE A MORT

ERNST
KALTENBRUNNER
CONDAMNE A MORT

ALFRED ROSENBERG
CONDAMNE A MORT

FRITZ SAUCKEL
CONDAMNE A MORT

RUDOLF HESS
PRISON A VIE

ERICH RAEDER
PRISON A VIE

WALTER FUNK
PRISON A VIE

HANS FRANK
CONDAMNE A MORT

ARTHUR
VON SEYSS-INQUART
CONDAMNE A MORT

ALBERT SPEER
20 ANS DE PRISON

CONSTANTIN
VON NEURATH
15 ANS DE PRISON

HJALMAR SCHACHT
ACQUITTE

HANS FRITSCHE
ACQUITTE

FRANZ VON PAPEN
ACQUITTE

KARL DOENITZ
10 ANS DE PRISON

BALDUR VON SCHIRACH
20 ANS DE PRISON

The twenty-one Nazi war criminals tried at Nuremberg with their sentences: CONDAMNÉ À MORT means "condemned to death"; PRISON À VIE means "life imprisonment"; 20 ANS DE PRISON means "20 years in prison" (etc.); ACQUITTÉ means "acquitted."

© Rue des Archives

The Nuremberg Trials

Twenty-four Nazis accused of the gravest war crimes were initially supposed to be brought before the Nuremberg tribunal. Eventually, twenty-one were tried, between November 20, 1945, and October 1, 1946, over the course of more than four hundred hearings; twelve were condemned to death (including one in absentia), ten of whom were hanged the night of October 16, 1946. Goering had succeeded in committing suicide shortly before. Numerous other trials followed at Nuremberg to consider the gravest criminal aspects of Nazism. ■

The Tokyo Trials

In order to implement the Potsdam Agreement of July 1945, which called for trials of Japanese war criminals, General MacArthur was directed to establish the International Military Tribunal for the Far East (IMTFE). The tribunal was composed of eleven judges, each representing one of the victorious Allied countries. MacArthur named former U.S. assistant attorney general Joseph Keenan chief prosecutor and an Australian, Sir William Webb, the tribunal's president.

The Tokyo trials lasted two and a half years, from May 3, 1946, to November 12, 1948, and comprised 818 hearings followed by seven months of deliberations. Of the twenty-eight accused who appeared before the court, seven were executed by hanging.

Following an agreement negotiated with MacArthur, the emperor and the imperial family were not threatened with prosecution or indicted; Hirohito's immunity was judged necessary to the security and success of the American occupation.

The members of Unit 731, which undertook secret medical and biological/chemical warfare experiments on human subjects in China, likewise remained unindicted: the tribunal did not even mention them during the hearings. Doubtless on account of the bombing of Hiroshima and Nagasaki, the notion of crimes against humanity was also never addressed. ∎

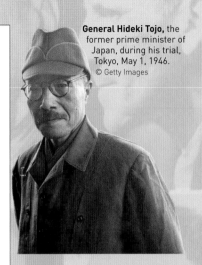

General Hideki Tojo, the former prime minister of Japan, during his trial, Tokyo, May 1, 1946.
© Getty Images

The Tokyo war crimes trials, which took place from May 1946 to November 1948. © NARA

Mohandas Karamchand Gandhi, father of Indian independence, known as Mahatma, "great soul."
© Rue des Archives

Goumiers (Moroccan soldiers who served in auxiliary units attached to the French Army of Africa) march along the Champs-Élysées in Paris on June 18, 1945, in a parade commemorating General Charles de Gaulle's Appeal of June 18, 1940.
© ECPAD

The Aspirations and Demands of Colonized Peoples

The weakening of Europe after World War II undermines the claims asserted by the colonial powers, but it cannot alone explain the worldwide emancipation movements that surge among colonized peoples. The principles of freedom advanced by the Allies throughout the conflict, the participation of colonial troops during the war, and the role of the United Nations, which quickly becomes a public platform for anticolonialism, all increase support for independence among the colonies' local elites. In India, Gandhi's Congress Party demands an end to colonial status in 1942, and in 1943 Fehrat Abbas proclaims the Manifesto of the Algerian People. ■

Soldier of the 4th Regiment of Moroccan Infantry during a decoration ceremony.
© ECPAD

Soldiers of the 17th Autonomous Battalion of Senegalese infantry, held as prisoners of war by the Germans in 1940. Their uniforms date from World War I: long greatcoats and the M15 Adrian helmet, the first modern steel military helmet.
© ECPAD

A regiment of Spahis (light cavalry recruited from the indigenous peoples of French colonies in Algeria, Tunisia, and Morocco) on parade in Konstanz, Germany, during a farewell ceremony for the U.S. General Jacob Devers hosted by the French 1st Army under General Jean de Lattre de Tassigny, June 18, 1945.
© ECPAD

Léopold Sédar Senghor, an internationally renowned francophone poet and later the first president of Senegal, developed in his writings as a cultural theorist the concept of *négritude*, which asserted the distinctive value of African culture in dialogue with others, Senegal, 1949.
© Roger Viollet

"The 'Good Negro' is dead; the paternalists should mourn him. It's the hen who laid the golden eggs that they've killed. Three centuries of the slave trade, a century of occupation could not rob us of our dignity; all the catechisms drilled into us (and the rationalist versions are not any less imperialist than the religious ones) could not make us believe in our inferiority. We want to work together in dignity and honor, without which there is only 'Kollaboration' à la Vichy. We are fed up with empty words and the good Word, sick of them; we've had it with contemptuous sympathy; what we need is justice. . . .

This war has no meaning if it is not anti-Nazi. Germany has been beaten, but Nazism has not, not in France, and above all not in Africa. That's what one of my fellow nègres told me sadly the evening of May 8, that day of Victory, and we couldn't manage to laugh, because our joy was troubled: our dead were not appeased."

Léopold Sédar Senghor, in Esprit, July 1, 1945

Hungarian Jewish women and children arrive at Auschwitz-Birkenau, as documented by an SS photographer, 1944. From the album *Auschwitz.*
© AKG-images

Memory and History

Memory *and History*

Reflection on the uses of history and memory has become inseparable from knowledge and understanding of the past. Of particular importance is an examination of the ways in which nation states and communities with conflicting collective memories appropriate history and use it for their own purposes.

Uses of the Past: The Work of Memory and Lapses of Memory

GERMANY
The work of remembrance undertaken in Germany on the nation's historical responsibility for causing World War II and its tragic consequences is often cited as exemplary. However, among other constantly debated issues, the role of the Wehrmacht remains a question on which no consensus has emerged.

FRANCE
The active contribution of the Vichy government to Jewish persecution was for a long time passed over in silence: the French state's role was falsely reduced to implementing German policies under duress—and the kepi of a French gendarme was erased from a sequence of Alain Resnais's film *Night and Shadow*. The names of the Buchenwald and Dachau concentration camps symbolized in France the tragedy of the Shoah. The truth has been more widely recognized since the 1970s, and the social pressure of Jewish memory has driven this return to history.

JAPAN
After 1945, the Japanese government expressed its intention to adopt a policy of pacifism. The critical attitude toward Japanese memories of the war expressed by the country's leaders and its elites has encouraged much public questioning of Japan's conduct during the 1930s and '40s. However, recognition of the massacres and other atrocities committed by the Imperial Army is rejected by Japan's radical nationalist element and remains a sensitive and controversial question that weighs heavily upon Japan's relations with its neighbors. Profoundly influenced by the country's official pacifism, which clouds reflection on the past, the Japanese cannot agree on the necessity of drawing a clear connection between perpetrators and victims.

UKRAINE (FORMER SOVIET UNION)
Nearly 34,000 Jews were massacred by the Nazis in the ravine at Babi Yar, near Kiev, Ukraine, in the last days of September 1941. The monument erected nearby in 1976 does not identify the victims. Not until 1991, with the dedication of a new monument, was the event officially acknowledged and commemorated, with explicit reference to the facts of what took place there.

Victims' Memories: Questions and Complexities

THE BOMBING OF CIVILIAN TARGETS

The commemoration of the victims of Allied bombing in Germany, and in particular the case of Dresden, poses the problem of sufferings silenced or suppressed. Their appropriate recognition is impossible without a patient effort to remember and an indispensable return to history. Yet this process must never be allowed to furnish a pretext for the perversion of historical meaning that enables executioners to transform themselves into victims.

In another context entirely, and with all due allowances for the very different circumstances involved, deeply suppressed taboos have long inhibited acknowledgement of the civilian victims of the Allied bombing of Normandy. They deserve to take their rightful place in the history of the Liberation.

THE "MALGRÉ NOUS"

In January 1953, during the trial of twenty-one of the men responsible for the massacre of the inhabitants of Oradour-sur-Glane on June 10, 1944, France discovered the problem of the *malgré nous* (despite ourselves, against our will)—the 130,000 Alsatians and Mosellans forcibly conscripted into the Wehrmacht and, in a few cases (the youngest men), into the Waffen-SS, a handful of whom had participated in the slaughter at Oradour. Profoundly shocked by their guilty verdicts, but quickly granted amnesty despite violent protest in the Limousin region around Oradour, the *malgré nous* have never ceased to affirm that they too were, above all, victims of Nazism.

Controversies and Changing Truths

INACTION IN THE FACE OF GENOCIDE

Starting in 1942, the Allied authorities were repeatedly informed, first of the threat, then of the fact, of the Jewish genocide in Europe. Nonetheless, the Allies never responded with any concrete action on any scale to stop the massacres, and the possibility of bombing the railway lines leading to Auschwitz was rejected as unrealistic and too risky. For British and U.S. military leaders, priority had to be placed on the destruction of the German war machine. This policy must be placed in the general context of silence and incomprehension where some, today, see indifference. The subject remains controversial.

KATYN

Not until 1990 did the USSR admit Soviet responsibility for the deaths of thousands of Polish officers at Katyn, executed by the NKVD (the Soviet secret police) on orders from Stalin himself and the Politburo in 1940. The Katyn affair—the development of the cover-up, the complicity at the highest levels of state in exploiting it and perverting the truth—constitutes one of the strongest examples of the potential links between the denial of truth and the suppression of memory, and the political purposes to which these can be put to support official state lies.

THE "PARTISAN STRUGGLE"

The recognition of the legitimacy of armed resistance in the occupied countries during the war was not without contradictions. Thus, at

*"**History is in essence the science of change.** It by no means teaches that the past ever repeats itself, that what was yesterday will be tomorrow."*
Marc Bloch, from "One of the Vanquished Gives Evidence," in Strange Defeat: A Statement of Evidence Written in 1940

> **"History is a means of organizing the past in order to prevent its weighing too heavily on the shoulders of men.** *It is for the sake of life that history interrogates death."*
>
> Lucien Febvre, from A New Kind of History (selected essays)

>>> the very moment when France celebrated the sacrifices of the Resistance, the country was engaged in a ruthless war against the independence movements in its colonies. The bloody massacre in the town of Sétif, Algeria, in which thousands of Algerians were killed by French forces on May 8, 1945—one day after the formal end of World War II in Europe—is a tragic symbol of this paradox. The example of the partisan struggle also served equally as after-the-fact "justification" for anticolonial terrorist actions against civilians.

Such lapses are expressions of the general corruption entailed by total war, including a widespread openly expressed contempt for the laws of war. Those laws were nonetheless codified persistently between 1864 and 1949 in the successive Geneva Conventions and later augmented by several additional protocols.

The Meaning of Historical Events and the Lessons of the Past

RECONSIDERING THE SHOAH

The increasing significance accorded to the "Holocaust by bullets" in the destruction of European Jewry may lead to changes in the way we think about the process of annihilation. If the death camps symbolize the fundamental uniqueness of the Jewish genocide, the massacres carried out openly in broad daylight, sometimes with the willing participation of the local non-Jewish community, qualify the image of a historical event characterized by secrecy, coded references, concealment, and cover-up; by the impossibility of adequately representing the unspeakable; by industrialized death and bureaucratized murder.

THE ABSTRACTION OF MASS DEATH

Industrial rationalization, advanced technologies, mechanized war, speed, the remote targets of aerial bombing, the vague fate of civilian populations, and the monstrous number of victims are all factors that render the dead and their dying invisible, anonymous, and distant. These aspects of war are not all there is to total war, but they are among the distinct signs of an evolution in the idea of war itself. In particular, war on such terms no longer has anything in common with the trenches and artillery barrages, the rifles and bayonets, "going over the top" and the infantry wave attacks of World War I.

LIBERATION IN WEST AND EAST

For the former USSR and in the Western vision of history, the impact of the Allied victory in May 1945 and the crushing of Nazism were immense. Yet they do not occupy the same place in collective memory in the countries of Eastern Europe that remained in the Soviet sphere until the revolutions of 1989 to 1991. Where people in the West speak of Liberation, Eastern Europeans decry the beginning of a new form of occupation. If recognition of divergent memories of the event's meaning is a constituent element of European identity, Europeans in both East and West cannot avoid questioning the ambiguities and amnesia that such recognition may at the same time reveal.

JUSTICE AND HISTORY

The convening of the International Military Tribunal and the first postwar trials, as well as later trials of war crimes and crimes against humanity, responded to a fundamental need for justice. Their impact on public opinion is important; they possess incontestable pedagogical value and cleared the way for the founding of the international justice system, including the United Nations' International Court of Justice and the International Criminal Court, as well as the latter's specialized tribunals, such as the International Criminal Tribunal for the Former Yugoslavia.

On the other hand, we may question the view of history that such courts express via their ultimately reductive verdicts of guilty or not guilty, and question too the limitations of the "victors' justice" rendered at Nuremberg and perhaps even more so during the Tokyo trials.

GENOCIDES

The term *genocide* was coined by the Polish-Jewish lawyer Raphael Lemkin in 1943 and first appeared in print in his *Axis Rule in Occupied Europe: Laws of Occupation—Analysis of Government—Proposals for Redress* (1944). The term was legally defined by the UN in December 1948. Subsequently, the International Criminal Court, founded in 1998, defined the crime of genocide as referring only to mass killings ordered by a state or similar de facto power. Three genocides have been recognized by United Nations authorities: the Turkish genocide against its Armenian community in 1915–16; the Nazi genocide against the Jews and the Roma/Sinti; and the Hutu genocide against the Tutsi in Rwanda in 1994. The International Criminal Tribunal for the Former Yugoslavia characterized the 1995 killings in Bosnia as genocide, but numerous other instances of mass murder since 1945 have not been considered to constitute genocide. Such is the case of the Khmer Rouge, who killed 1.7 million Cambodians between 1975 and 1979.

D-Day and the Battle of Normandy

By Jean Quellien

British airborne troops prepare for takeoff during the night of June 5–6, 1945. The men smear their faces with black greasepaint or burned cork (sometimes even soot or oil) in order to be less visible at night.
© Imperial War Museum

British troops land on Gold Beach
on D-Day.
© NARA

The front lines in the Battle of Normandy

Cherbourg

Valognes

Montebourg

Sainte-Mère-Église

Sainte-Marie-du-Mont

Carentan

La-Haye-du-Puits

Sainteny

Coutances

Saint-Lô

Port-en-Bessin

Bayeux

Graye-sur-Mer

Carpiquet

Aunay-sur-Odon

Vire

Flers

Avranches

Pontaubault

Mortain

UTAH BEACH

POINTE DU HOC

OMAHA BEACH

Colleville-sur-Mer

Longues-sur-Mer

Arromanches

GOLD BEACH

Ver-sur-Mer

Courseulles-sur-Mer

JUNO BEACH

Hermanville-sur-Mer

SWORD BEACH

Ouistreham

Le Havre

Merville

Bénouville

Ranville

Caen

Pont l'Évêque

Lisieux

Elbeuf

Falaise

Trun

Chambois

Argentan

Alençon

❶ On June 6
❷ On June 30
❸ On August 1
❹ On August 15

Canadian propaganda poster.
© Library and Archives Canada

Preparations

A few days after the retreat from Dunkirk in June 1940, Britain's Prime Minister Winston Churchill declares defiantly, "We shall return!" It will be four years until Churchill's promise can be fulfilled, in June 1944. In 1940–41, the United Kingdom, alone in the war against the Third Reich, must think first of self-defense. But the year 1941 changes the course of the war with the entry of first the USSR into the conflict, then of the U.S., who will throw all their weight into the balance and tip the scales in the Allies' favor.

Meeting in Washington in December, Roosevelt and Churchill agree to work together to defeat the Third Reich. Eager to see the war ended quickly, the U.S., beginning in April 1942, offers two proposals for landings in France. But the British general staff rejects the first, which they judge too hazardous, and considers the second premature. A period of long and difficult negotiations between the two allies begins.

Two Allied Strategies

The British prudently advocate the bullfighter's strategy of wearing down the enemy by attacks at the edges of the German-held territory before launching a final assault. They succeed in persuading the other Allies to undertake a series of landings in the Mediterranean: first in North Africa, next in Sicily (Operation Avalanche), then in southern Italy. However, during the Casablanca Conference of January 1943 (with Roosevelt, Churchill, de Gaulle, and other representatives of the Free French Forces attending), the U.S. presses the other　**>>>**

One last tune on the warpipes before boarding.
© Imperial War Museum

Field Marshal Erwin Rommel inspects the Atlantic Wall.
© Bundesarchiv

>>> representatives to decide upon a great cross-Channel invasion for 1944 in order to be able to attack Germany more directly and hasten the Nazis' defeat.

Operation Overlord is now on track. Its first phase, the landing of troops on the beaches of Normandy, will be called Operation Neptune.

German Preparations: The Atlantic Wall

Hitler's decision to build the Wall of the Atlantic in December 1941 results from the evolution of his overall strategy. The commitment of the bulk of the German forces to the Eastern Front leaves German defenses dangerously undermanned in the West, which are now threatened by an anticipated Allied invasion.

Construction of the Wall begins in spring 1942. No less than 11 million metric tons of concrete will be needed to build 15,000 fortifications along 3,700 miles of coastline. The Nazis undertake an intense propaganda campaign, aimed above all at reassuring the German public of the Wall's invincibility.

In November 1943, Field Marshal Rommel is ordered by Hitler to inspect the Wall of the Atlantic. In January 1944, Rommel, who has recently been named commander of Army Group B, moves the group to Normandy to protect all the territory from the Netherlands to the Loire River, the area most threatened by Allied invasion. Rommel speeds up the completion of the Wall and notably orders that unprotected German artillery be placed inside thick concrete bunkers to shield it from aerial attack.

Rommel also increases the number of minefields and takes particular care with the defense of the Norman beaches, which are soon covered with obstacles designed to block or destroy Allied landing barges.

The Invasion of France: Where and When?

In May 1943, at the conference code-named Trident, in Washington, DC, the Allies decide to invade France in May 1944, while leaving open the question of exactly where the landings will take place.

Considering the limits of Allied air cover, which must fly from English airfields, two areas are possible. The Germans expect, logically, an assault in the Pas-de-Calais, the point closest to the English coast, and consequently build their strongest defenses there. The coast of the Seine Estuary, between Le Havre and Cherbourg, farther from Britain and therefore apparently less threatened, is left less well protected.

Valuing the element of surprise above all, the Allied chiefs of staff, meeting in Québec City in August 1943 (at the conference code-named Quadrant), choose the beaches of Lower Normandy. Much remains to be done to encourage the Germans to remain secure in their conviction that the invasion will land in the Pas-de-Calais; this will be the aim of the campaign of deception code-named Operation Fortitude.

BACK 'EM UP

BUY *EXTRA* BONDS

This American poster urges citizens to buy the war bonds that will finance the Normandy invasion. The preparations for Operation Overlord require an increase in military production, including aircraft, tanks, artillery, and ships. The dynamism of American and Canadian factories has to compensate for the exhaustion of British industry. The war effort is financed in effect by borrowing from the two countries' citizens through their purchase of war bonds.
© Caen Memorial

Bombing of the railway station at Tourcoing, on the Belgian border, by bi-motor Boston bombers of the RAF 2nd Tactical Air Force.
© Imperial War Museum

A Phoenix caisson under construction on the banks of the Tamise. Sunk end-to-end, the concrete caissons will form sea walls to protect the Mulberry artificial harbors. © Imperial War Museum

Allied Logistics: The Construction of Artificial Harbors

After the raid on Dieppe in August 1942 (Operation Jubilee), Hitler ordered the fortification of the French harbors on the Atlantic coast, certain that the Allies would attempt to take control of them in case of any future assault.

Once again doing the opposite of what they have led the Germans to expect, the Allies abandon the idea of a frontal attack on the heavily fortified ports of Le Havre and Cherbourg and decide to land on the beaches.

However, the landing of men in great numbers together with great quantities of matériel demands specially adapted infrastructure. From this necessity is born the idea of constructing artificial harbors, all of whose parts will be built in England, floated across the Channel, and assembled on site.

The Allied plan to create two artificial harbors (code-named Mulberries), one each in the American and British landing areas.

The Allied Bombing of France

In spring 1944, Allied aviation increases its bombing raids over France, striving to reduce as much as possible the German army's capacity for counterattack on D-Day.

Railway infrastructure, coastal artillery batteries, radar stations, air bases, and railway and automotive bridges are all attacked in turn, as well as the secret launch sites for the V1 flying bombs and V2 missiles (the world's first rockets) hidden along the French coast.

The bombing campaign causes the deaths of numerous French civilians, and both the occupying Nazi regime and the Vichy government make every effort **>>>**

>>> to exploit the death toll in an effort to turn public opinion against the Allies.

Revision of the Plan

In January 1944, General Eisenhower is appointed Supreme Commander of Operation Overlord with, among his deputies, Britain's Field Marshal Montgomery.

The plan developed in 1943 by the French-American staff under British Lieutenant-General Frederick E. Morgan, Chief of Staff to the Supreme Allied Commander (COSSAC), seems to Eisenhower and Montgomery too small in scale, and they decide to increase the number of troops involved. They decide further to enlarge the landing area by adding a beach at either end, one extending to the mouth of the Orne River and another on the coast of the Cotentin Peninsula, in order to enable a more rapid conquest of Cherbourg. The modification of the plan for D-Day requires a delay while additional troops and matériel are assembled. For this reason, the landings are postponed until the beginning of June.

Several factors determine the choice of D-Day itself: the need for a full moon the night before to aid the initial paratrooper attack, which will be followed by the seaborne assault at dawn on a rising tide, in order to reduce as much as possible the danger of the traps laid by Rommel on the beaches. Consequently, the date of June 5 is chosen, with June 6 or 7 as backup dates.

Hobart's Funnies. In order to deal with the specific problems of the Normandy landings, especially the challenges posed by German defenses, special armored vehicles are obviously necessary. The task of designing them falls to Major-General Percy Hobart (LEFT), an armored warfare specialist, military engineer, and commander of the British 79th Armored Division. The odd-looking modified tanks that emerge from his fertile imagination are nicknamed "Hobart's Funnies."
© Imperial War Museum

A strategic planning session in Great Britain around a model of the site of the D-Day landings.
© Imperial War Museum

Members of the Allied general staffs meet to plan Operation Overlord in the library at Southwick Park, in southern England. FROM LEFT TO RIGHT: Lieutenant General Omar Bradley, Commanding General of the U.S. 1st Army; Admiral Bertram Ramsey, Allied Naval Commander-in-Chief; RAF Air Chief Marshal Arthur Tedder, Deputy Supreme Commander; General Dwight D. Eisenhower, Supreme Commander in charge of Operation Overlord; Field Marshal Bernard Montgomery, Deputy Supreme Commander and commander of the 21st Army Group, which comprises all the Allied ground forces for Operation Overlord; Air Chief Marshal Trafford Leigh-Mallory, Commander-in-Chief of the Allied Expeditionary Air Forces for the Normandy invasion; and General Walter Bedell Smith, Eisenhower's chief of staff.
© Imperial War Museum

American paratroopers
en route to the Cotentin
Peninsula.
© NARA

D-Day

On June 4, the weather deteriorates and the forecast for June 5 is catastrophic: violent winds, low cloud cover, very rough seas. Eisenhower and his general staff, discouraged, decide to postpone the invasion.

But toward dawn the next day, while the storm continues to rage, the north Atlantic weather stations begin to predict calmer seas for June 6. After going around the table quickly with his staff, Eisenhower makes the fateful decision: "Okay, let's go!" It is 4:15 A.M. on June 5. Tuesday, June 6, will be the historic day.

The Germans, however, convinced that the storm will last for some time, call off their regular sea patrols and aerial reconnaissance between Le Havre and Cherbourg. The immense Allied armada, which has been assembled throughout the day on the June 5, will be able to approach the Norman coast unmolested.

General Bradley will say later that the sudden turn in the weather was the Allies' "Trojan horse."

The Paratrooper Assault
The mission of the paratroopers is to secure the two flanks of the landing area. In the west, the U.S. 82nd and 101st Airborne Divisions are assigned to take possession of the important road junction at the village of Sainte-Mère-Église, gain a foothold on the other side of the Merderet River, and secure the exit routes from Utah Beach.

In the east, the British 6th Airborne is tasked, first, with taking the bridges over the Orne River and the Orne Canal, in order to enable the troops who land at Sword Beach to cross them; second, with destroying the bridges over the Dives River, to delay the arrival of German reinforcements heading for the Allied beachhead; and finally, with neutralizing the artillery battery at Merville.

Owing to the unpredictability of their drops, both paratroopers and glider pilots are widely dispersed and often land far from their targets; some are dropped too fast or too low to survive landing. Many of the strays are captured by the Germans; others are killed in combat or drown in the marshlands flooded on Rommel's orders. Nonetheless, the men accomplish every one of their missions.

Utah Beach

At 6:30 A.M., the U.S. 4th Infantry Division under General Raymond O. Barton, supported by amphibious tanks, lands below the dunes of La Madeleine, the beach at Sainte-Marie-du-Mont.

Fortunately, the division's barges are driven by the coastal currents more than a mile south of their predicted landing site, where they would have faced much greater danger. German resistance there, depleted by aerial and naval bombardment, is weak. By early afternoon, the 4th is able to link up with the 101st Airborne.

Pointe du Hoc

The 230 men of the 2nd Ranger Battalion under Lieutenant-Colonel James E. Rudder are entrusted with one of D-Day's most perilous missions. They have to neutralize an important artillery battery that threatens both Utah and Omaha beaches, situated atop a rocky spur 100 feet above the sea.

Since they cannot be certain that pre-liminary bombing has silenced the battery, the Rangers must climb the cliff face in order to take it; this they do quickly and without too many losses, believing that a furious battle with the battery's garrison next awaits them.

After securing their position, Rudder's men are astonished to discover that all the guns have been removed to protect them from aerial attack. However, encircled by counterattacking German troops, the Rangers will not be rescued until two days later. By that time, only 90 will remain in battle condition; 80 of their comrades will have perished.

Omaha Beach

Omaha Beach lies on a bay about five miles wide between Vierville and Colleville-sur-Mer, overlooked here and there by cliffs and surmounted by a steep slope riddled with artillery, mortars, and machine gun emplacements.

The Allied military leaders are aware of the danger of being trapped on the beach during the assault. Yet Omaha is the only possible landing place that avoids leaving a yawning gap in the landing zone between Utah and Gold beaches. Poorly aimed aerial and naval bombardment has left the German defenses nearly intact, and they have been moreover reinforced by the arrival, undetected by the Allies, of the exceptionally strong German 352nd Infantry Division.

On the morning of June 6, the men of

The voices of Radio TSF, broadcasting from radios like this one.
Caen Memorial

RADIO AT WAR: "PLEASE LISTEN TO A FEW PERSONAL MESSAGES . . ."

As a means of communication between the Resistance in France and the Allied forces in London, radio plays a crucial role on D-Day. Contrary to what is widely believed, the famous couplet by poet Paul Verlaine broadcast over the BBC on June 1 —"Les sanglots longs des violons d'automne . . ." (The long sobs of autumn's violins . . .)—and on June 5—"Bercent mon coeur d'une langueur monotone" (Rock my heart to sleep with monotonous languor) is not the main coded message announcing the Allied landings, but merely one message among many others. Messages broadcast on June 1 are intended to put the various French Resistance organizations on alert. The 210 or so messages broadcast for 16 minutes on June 5 around 9:15 P.M. give the order to the French Resistance to go into action immediately throughout the country. The essential objective is, by means of ambush and sabotage, to block as much as possible the movement of German troops toward the beachhead established by the Allies. The mobilization of the Maquis, who are numerous in the south of France, is intended to pin down as many German troops as possible there, far from Normandy.

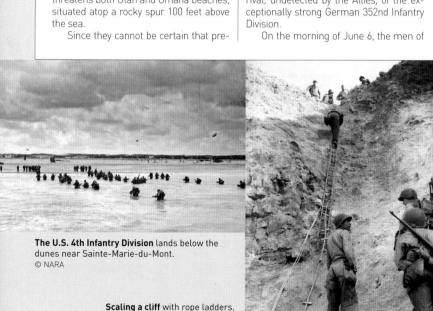

The U.S. 4th Infantry Division lands below the dunes near Sainte-Marie-du-Mont.
© NARA

Scaling a cliff with rope ladders.
© NARA

the U.S. 1st Infantry Division, commanded by Major-General Clarence Huebner, and the 29th Infantry Division, commanded by Major-General Charles Gerhardt, endure a veritable slaughter at "Bloody Omaha." Pinned down on the beach amid a field of corpses and charred wreckage, it takes the GIs nearly six hours to extricate themselves from the morass, climb the slopes above the beach, and reach the plateau behind it.

By nightfall, the Americans have penetrated barely a mile inland—a small gain for such heavy losses.

Gold Beach
The British 50th (Northumbrian) Infantry Division under Major-General Douglas Alexander Graham lands near Asnelles and Ver-sur-Mer at 7:25 A.M., about an hour later than the Americans at Utah and Omaha Beaches, owing to variations in the speed of the rising tide. German resistance is strong at the far ends of the landing zone, but the German emplacements are weak in the middle of the zone and cannot prevent a British breakthrough inland. By the evening of June 6, advance units of the 50th reach the outskirts of Bayeux, which they will take the next day without a fight.

Meanwhile, the 1st Battalion of the Royal Hampshire Regiment, a component of the 50th, hugging the coast, advances to take Arromanches, where one of the two Allied artificial harbors is to be built, by late afternoon.

A landing barge heads toward Omaha Beach.
© NARA

British troops land at Gold Beach.
© Library and Archives Canada

The Canadian 3rd Infantry Division lands at Bernières.
© Library and Archives Canada

Juno Beach

The sector between Courseulles and Saint-Aubin is assigned to the Canadian 3rd Infantry Division under Major-General Roderick Keller, supported by the No. 48 (Royal Marine) Commando battalion.

Owing to the presence of coastal reefs, which make navigation difficult, the Canadian assault landing craft are delayed in arriving on the beach. Landing at high tide, they crash against the obstacles Rommel has laid, leading to heavy losses and a dangerous pileup of men and matériel on the sand.

Despite hard combat, the Canadians succeed in establishing a solid bridgehead and in linking up with the British forces landed at Gold Beach. However, they have yet to attain two of their objectives: National Highway 13, and the air base at Carpiquet.

Sword Beach

The sector west of the mouth of the Orne River and the Orne Canal, between Langrune and Ouistreham, is solidly fortified. However, the British 3rd Infantry Division under Major-General Thomas Rennie is backed up by two special Commando Brigades.

The British land below Hermanville and Colleville. They take Ouistreham only after fierce fighting, where the commandos of the. No. 1 French Troop of the No. 10 (Inter-Allied) Commando (also called the 1re Compagnie de Fusiliers Marins or 1st Company of Naval Rifles) particularly distinguish themselves.

In the afternoon, the 1st Special Service Brigade under Lieutenant-Colonel Simon Fraser, Lord Lovat, reaches the bridges at Ranville and Bénouville and links up with the paratroopers. However, the 4th Brigade barely manages to take Lion and Luc-sur-Mer, leaving a gap between Sword and Juno beaches through which a detachment of the 21st Panzer Division is able, by evening, to reach the sea—though it immediately turns back.

In the middle of the sector, the bulk of the 3rd Division, slowed down by fortified German positions, stops a few miles from Caen, without having succeeded in taking the city as they are expected to.

The Evening of June 6

Even if all of D-Day's objectives have not been achieved, by the evening of June 6, the landings are considered a success: 155,000 men are on the ground in Normandy, together with 20,000 vehicles.

Allied losses, considerably fewer than anticipated, comprise slightly fewer than 10,000 men killed, wounded, or taken prisoner, including 3,000 dead.

The Atlantic Wall, the outermost ramparts of Hitler's "Fortress Europe," has been breached in a single day. The German coastal batteries have sunk only one ship, the destroyer USS *Curry*, off Utah Beach. A few other ships have been destroyed by mines and torpedo-launching boats.

The German coastal defenses have proven less effective than expected, unable to block the Allied advance over the beaches to any great extent, except at Omaha, where the GIs are still fighting with their backs to the sea. Everywhere else, the Allies have secured bridgeheads six miles or more inland.

Gathering and identifying the dead at Omaha Beach.
© NARA

British Commando insignia.
Caen Memorial

Bombing of transport links
by Allied aviation.
© U.S. Army

A wounded German soldier.
© Bundesarchiv

Days of Decision

D-Day is a success. But D-Day is in itself by no means decisive. The fate of Operation Overlord will depend from this point forward on the ability of the two opposing armies to build up their forces.

In theory, the Germans have the advantage: if the Allies cannot prevent them, the Wehrmacht can, within only one or two days, send toward Normandy some twenty divisions currently standing within a radius of 250 miles around the Allied bridgehead. The Germans thus enjoy a clear advantage over their adversaries, whose reinforcements, arriving by sea, will come more slowly—a factor that might allow Rommel to drive the Allied troops back into the ocean. For the Allies, it is thus essential to use every means available to slow the arrival of German reinforcements. In addition to the French Resistance, the Allies will take full advantage of their crushing aerial superiority, while continuing to benefit from the lasting effects of the advance deception operations code-named Fortitude.

The Destruction of Norman Cities and Towns

In order to prevent German reinforcements passing through them, the Allies have planned to reduce to rubble a certain number of cities and towns that contain important transport junctions beyond the Allied bridgeheads.

On the evening of June 6, around 8 P.M., Pont-l'Évêque, Lisieux, Flers, Condé-sur-Noireau, Vire, Saint-Lô, and Coutances are ravaged by U.S. Air Force bombers. When the resulting destruction is judged insufficient, the RAF Bomber Command strikes on the night of June 6–7. Argentan is added to the list, as well as Caen, which the Allies have failed to take as planned during the day. Casualties are heavy, with nearly 3,000 civilians killed—and results

that will later be revealed as of limited value from a tactical point of view.

Hell on Earth: Germans Troops on the Roads of Normandy

Preoccupied with their defense of the German heartland from long-range Allied bombing and chronically short of fuel, the Luftwaffe is almost entirely absent from the Battle of Normandy. The Allies own the skies. On the Norman roads, German convoys live in terror of the appearance of the dreaded Allied *Jabos*, from the German *Jäger Bomber* (hunter-bomber). Armed with onboard cannons, machine guns, and bombs or rockets, aircraft such as the P-47 Thunderbolts and B-26 Marauders dance an infernal ballet in the skies over Normandy, seeming to descend out of nowhere on their prey, leaving behind death and destruction. To avoid total annihilation, German convoys must resort to heavy camouflage with cut branches and to moving only during the short June nights.

Without question, the Allies' tactical use of aviation to slow the German reinforcements proves to be much more effective than the destruction of French cities and towns.

Extending the Bridgehead

Ten days after D-Day, the Allies have won the battle for the successful buildup of forces. They now enjoy a numerical superiority that they will maintain until the end of the war, and which will allow them to keep the Germans permanently on the defensive. By June 8, forces landed at Sword and Juno Beaches have linked up; by June 9, the troops landed at Gold and Omaha have done likewise; and finally, by June 12, with the taking of Carentan, those landed at Omaha and Utah beaches do also. From now on, the bridgehead

occupies a continuous swath of territory 56 miles wide. Yet for all this, the Battle of Normandy is only in its beginning stages. The Allies will have to spend two months in fierce combat to win it, in the face of ferocious German resistance.

A Strategic Priority: The Capture of Cherbourg

For the Americans, Cherbourg represents a vital strategic goal. Its broad deepwater harbor will enable the Allies to unload cargo ships bringing men, matériel, and provisions directly from the U.S. necessary for the success of Operation Overlord.

From the bridgehead at Utah Beach, Brigadier General Joseph "Lightning Joe" Lawton Collins, commander of the U.S. VII Corps, launches an offensive that isolates the Cotentin Peninsula at its base on June 18. His troops move north rapidly, liberating in passing the ruins of Valognes. By June 21, the Americans have arrived at Cherbourg. Hitler's Cherbourg Fortress extends on both sides of the city along a 19-mile stretch of seafront, including a dozen heavy batteries,

and proves to be formidable, as the Germans show in a duel with American ships massed offshore, but successfully kept at bay. The Fortress's inland defenses, built in haste, are weaker. The battle, begun on June 22, is brief. By the next day, the first defensive ring is breached. On the 25th, the GIs sweep through the city streets. On the 26th, the old Fort du Roule, overlooking the city, falls, and the German garrison soon surrenders.

The citizens of Cherbourg rejoice as the city's bells, silent for four years, ring out to welcome the Liberation. The city has suffered little in the battle, and the few thousand Cherbourgeois who escaped the forced evacuation of 1943 give free rein to their joy.

Only one shadow falls over the scene: the sorry state of the port, which the Germans have methodically sabotaged during the last few days preceding the city's fall. The navigation channels and the slips are full of scuttled wrecks and mines; the docks and the harbor station have been blown up; and the port's canal locks, railway links, and turning bridge are likewise destroyed.

An American soldier poses in front of road signs installed by the Germans near Cherbourg.
© NARA

A runway is surfaced with tarmac for American B-10 bombers near Plumetôt.
© Imperial War Museum

Logistics

In the Allied armies of 1944, combat troops represent about half of total military personnel; the other half comprises men and women who fulfill logistical tasks whose importance is often underestimated, though it is in fact no less fundamental.

During the Battle of Normandy, the Allies land 2 million men, 440,000 vehicles, and 3 million metric tons of munitions, provisions, and fuel.

Noncombat personnel construct about 50 forward airfields and two artificial harbors; put the port of Cherbourg in working order; maintain matériel of all kinds; and repair telephone lines, roads, railways, and bridges; not to mention staffing the field hospitals that care for the numerous wounded soldiers.

These facts alone highlight the importance of military logistics in the Normandy campaign—one of the keys to victory.

Construction of Allied Airfields in Normandy

Time lost in flying back and forth to England, which has to be added to every flight, limits the range of Allied aviation and threatens to restrict the length of the fighters' sorties and thus the Allies' control of the Norman skies.

In order to address this problem, the invasion plan foresees from the beginning the construction of airfields at the bridgehead as rapidly as possible in order to ensure maximum air cover.

The first runways, intended for emergency landings, become operational by June 7 and 8. Within a few weeks, some fifty Advanced Landing Grounds (ALGs) have been laid out, mainly in the Bassin area around Bayeux and on the Cotentin Peninsula. They are designated with the letter *A* for American and *B* for British bases, followed by a number (except for 13). The Allies' airfields each **>>>**

>>> cover an area of about 500 acres, with runways usually about 1,300 yards long, and additional cleared areas for parking and maintaining aircraft, hangars, and other buildings all adjacent. The bases are assigned either to the U.S. 9th Air Force or the RAF's 2nd Tactical Air Force, which are principally responsible for supporting the Allied ground forces.

During the Battle of Normandy, Allied aviation will complete a total of nearly 200,000 sorties and will play a crucial role in the Allied victory.

Construction of the Two Artificial Harbors

The Allies construct two artificial harbors off the Norman coast: one, codenamed Mulberry A, in the U.S. sector, off Omaha Beach; and the other, Mulberry B, in the British sector, off Gold Beach, near Arromanches. Every element of the harbors is built in England and floated across the Channel behind the invasion fleet before being assembled at the two chosen sites.

Only ten days after D-Day, the two ports are both partly operational. Each comprises about six miles of flexible steel roadways (code-named Whales) that float on steel or concrete pontoons (Beetles). Lines of scuttled ships (Goose-berries) protect the harbors from the sea, together with massive sunken caissons (Phoenixes) and floating breakwaters (Bombardons).

Between June 19 and 21 a powerful storm damages Mulberry B and destroys Mulberry A. The British harbor, repaired with elements salvaged from the ruins of Mulberry A, will make history, while the latter, abandoned, will be entirely forgotten.

In order to unload men and matériel at Omaha, the Americans resort to less sophisticated methods (grounding ships onshore, off-loading, and then refloating them on the next high tide) that in the end prove more effective, with results far superior to those obtained by Mulberry B at Arromanches.

Repair of the Port of Cherbourg, the Harbor of Liberation

When American forces take possession of Cherbourg at the end of June, German sabotage has rendered the port totally unusable. In the short term, it is thus impossible to unload ships arriving from the U.S. as planned.

Undiscouraged, the teams of Allied engineers get to work immediately, exemplifying the motto adopted by American Seabees (the construction battalions of the U.S. Navy's Civil Engineer >>>

ABOVE, UPPER: **American soldiers unload war matériel** at Cherbourg. © NARA

ABOVE, LOWER: **The unloading docks** of the Allies' two Mulberry artificial harbors are formed from huge steel platforms with giant pierheads, called Spuds; they are jacked up and down on 100-foot-high piles that rest on the seafloor, buoyed by the rising and falling tides.
© Imperial War Museum

The unloading of locomotives and trucks relies partly on specially outfitted ferries.
© Imperial War Museum

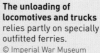

Phoenix caissons cross the English Channel, pulled by tugboats. They will form the main barrier for the artificial harbors that protects the docks from the sea; once pulled into place, they are filled with seawater and sunk to the seafloor.
© Imperial War Museum

THE ROLE OF THE PORT OF CHERBOURG IN RAILWAY RECONSTRUCTION

The French railway system has been devastated by Allied aerial bombing and Resistance sabotage in the months leading up to D-Day. Rolling stock has been especially hard hit: of the 17,000 locomotives that the SNCF (the French national railway) boasted before the war, no more than 3,000 remain in working order.

If the Allies are to follow the success of Operation Overlord with an advance toward the German frontier, it is imperative that the railway system be restored. For a period lasting several months, the port of Cherbourg will be the only harbor available to the Allies that can handle the unloading of the heavy matériel involved.

>>> Corps) during the war: "The difficult we do immediately. The impossible takes a little longer."

In only a few weeks, the port of Cherbourg is operational once again. On July 16, 1944, the first four Liberty Ships arrive from the U.S. in the port. Since the wharves are not yet repaired, the ships have to lie at anchor in the roadstead, from where their cargo is unloaded and transferred to the Place Napoléon in town, the main thoroughfare behind the harbor.

By the end of July, the Liberty Ships are unloading 4,000 metric tons of cargo a day, a rate that reaches 24,000 tons a day by autumn, far exceeding expectations and, for a time, even outpacing the port of New York.

The work of unloading the ships is mainly accomplished by porter battalions principally comprising African American soldiers. Forbidden through most of the war from serving in combat because of the segregation of U.S. forces, African American men are assigned in large numbers to logistics.

Caring for Tens of Thousands of the Wounded

On D-Day, wounded soldiers are attended to on the beaches themselves by military medical teams. However, an entire medical infrastructure is rapidly put in place at the bridgehead, from first-aid stations to veritable hospitals with many hundreds of beds installed under tents.

During the Battle of Normandy, Allied hospitals will care for 185,000 wounded service personnel, not counting tens of thousands of German soldiers and a many civilians as well. But the majority of those wounded at the front in Normandy are transferred to England, where >>>

An injured American is carried on a stretcher by German prisoners of war.
© NARA

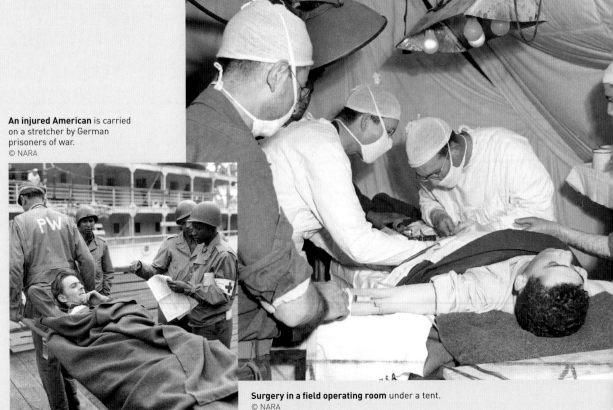

Surgery in a field operating room under a tent.
© NARA

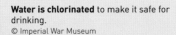

Water is chlorinated to make it safe for drinking.
© Imperial War Museum

Setting up a telephone exchange near Cherbourg.
© NARA

>>> they can benefit from more appropriate care or better housing for long convalescence.

Depending on the seriousness of their injuries, the wounded are evacuated either by plane from designated forward air bases, or by ambulance ships leaving from Cherbourg and Arromanches.

Finding Millions of Gallons of Water

The architects of Operation Overlord could not neglect the essential problem of providing water for the invasion. Fortunately, Normandy does not suffer from a lack of water.

However, the amount of water needed by an Allied army comprising hundreds of thousands of men is considerable: for drinking, bathing, laundry, hospitals, and cleaning vehicles, not to mention wetting down runways.

While village wells can supply part of the need, several pumping stations have to be installed in local rivers; water is also drawn from sources carefully identified, before D-Day, on geological maps.

Re-establishing Communications

Aerial bombing, artillery barrages, and sabotage committed by the Resistance and the retreating Germans have all left the French communications systems in a dreadful state. Allied engineers must repair them as fast as possible to facilitate movement not only of Allied troops, but of civilians as well.

Restoring water lines in the park of the Château de Creullet.
© Imperial War Museum

MILITARY DEPOTS INVADE THE NORMAN COUNTRYSIDE

Over the course of summer 1944, the Norman countryside is covered with enormous depots in which munitions, artillery, vehicles, spare tires, crates of rations, fuel, and other materials are stored. As General Eisenhower remarks, the biggest resupply depot in human history now stretches from Cherbourg to Caen.

A forward emergency medical team takes charge of the wounded.
© Imperial War Museum

The German Tiger heavy tank, a steel monster weighing 55 metric tons.
© Bundesarchiv

The Allies Prevail

BRITISH AND CANADIAN OPERATIONS

Confronting the Panzers

Montgomery is unable to liberate Caen on June 6 as planned. Since D-Day, he is stalled before the veritable wall of steel and fire thrown up before his troops by the several Panzer divisions that arrive to reinforce the German forces. In vain, Montgomery attempts several times to attack the city from the west, trying to take it with a turning attack. Every attempt ends in failure, including Operation Epsom, a broad offensive launched in late June.

All the same, by maintaining the initiative in the Battle of Caen, Montgomery does succeed in reducing the Germans' redoubtable Panzer divisions to a defensive role, thus preventing them from mounting any large-scale counterattack.

The Failure of Operation Epsom

June 26 sees the launching of the largest Allied offensive since D-Day. Montgomery sends 90,000 men, 600 tanks, and 700 pieces of artillery into action. Their objective: to cross the Odon River, then the Orne River south of Caen, in order to take the city from the back. However, south of the Orne, the Allied attack is soon broken by the arrival of armored SS divisions called up from the Eastern Front. From this point forward, pitched battles will ensue lasting for weeks around hill 112, with a series of attacks and counterattacks that will prove equally lethal for both sides.

The Shadow of Trench Warfare Hovers Over Caen

As June progresses, the British and Canadian forces barely advance. In fairness, they are confronted by the cream of the German army, including the majority of the German armored divisions engaged on the Norman front, reinforced by battalions of the Wehrmacht's lethal Tiger heavy tanks. Unable to more forward, the troops on both sides dig in: "Dig or die." The shadow of trench warfare hovers over Caen.

The situation causes increasing tension at the heart of the Allied leadership. The Americans, buoyed by their conquest of Cherbourg, do not hesitate to criticize Montgomery for his slowness. However, it will not be long before the Americans themselves will run into still greater difficulties in their own sector.

July 9: Caen Falls at Last

After a month-long siege and the failure of all his flanking maneuvers, Montgomery decides to return to a frontal assault on the city. The final offensive on July 4 is preceded by an attack, west of Caen, on the village of Carpiquet and its airfield, the site of fierce battle.

On the evening of July 7, a massive aerial bombardment opens a breach in the German defenses north of Caen. With Canadian troops moving from the west and British forces up the center of the front, on July 9 the Allies finally enter the city, which they find in ruins.

The German troops retreat, but take up solid positions across the Orne, on the right bank, which will not be liberated until ten days later.

July 19: The Right Bank is Liberated

On July 18, Montgomery launches Operation Goodwood. Following massive bombardment of the German lines southwest of Caen, nearly a thousand tanks attack across open country, heading for the village of Falaise.

However, the German defenses, positioned securely and in depth, soon put a halt to the offensive, which is called off after two days, with a considerable number of Allied tanks lost. The deadlock has not been broken.

The Allies only gain is the liberation of the right bank of Caen by the Canadians, assisted by the French Forces of the Interior (FFI), in an aspect of Goodwood code-named Operation Atlantic.

JUNE 14, 1944: DE GAULLE LANDS IN NORMANDY

On the early afternoon of June 14, General Charles de Gaulle, accompanied by his closest aids, crosses the Channel on board *La Combattante*, returning to France for the first time since escaping to London in June 1940.

De Gaulle's main goal is to assert the authority of the Provisional Government of the French Republic over the territories liberated by the Allies.

After visiting General Montgomery, de Gaulle moves on to Bayeux, then stops for a few moments at Isigny and Grandchamp before leaving Normandy on the evening of this historic day.

If he does not truly intend to install in France an Allied Military Government of Occupied Territories (AMGOT) regime like the one already set up in Italy, President Roosevelt equally has no intention of allowing France to fall into the hands of de Gaulle, whose claim to represent the French people Roosevelt questions.

However, the enthusiastic welcome de Gaulle receives in Bayeux incontestably proves the general's popular legitimacy and counters objections to his claims; this leads, shortly thereafter, to official Allied recognition of the Provisional Government.

Canadian troops enter Caen at last, after a month-long siege.
Caen Memorial

General de Gaulle prepares to leave Courseulles for the Chateau de Creullet, General Montgomery's headquarters.
Caen Memorial

U.S. OPERATIONS

Hell Among the Hedgerows

In early July, following the capture of Cherbourg, U.S. forces relaunch their southern offensive toward Coutances and Saint-Lô, only to be checked by vigorous resistance from German forces who know how to take perfect advantage of the local terrain. The typical *bocage* landscape of Normandy, where farmers traditionally define their fields not with stone or wooden fences but with living natural fences made from dense, high hedgerows, not only presents attackers with a series of small open fields hard to cross safely and enclosed by nearly impenetrable barriers, but it affords defenders a plethora of entrenched defensive positions in the ditches at the foot of the hedges.

The U.S. material advantage of greater numbers of men and machines is of little effect in such terrain. Attempting to crash through the high hedgerows, the Sherman tanks belly up, exposing their unarmored undersides while their own guns point skyward, making them easy targets for the German infantry's *Panzerschreck* (88 mm antitank rocket launcher)—one direct hit is usually enough to take out any Allied armored vehicle. At the same time, the Allied hunter bombers encounter great difficulties in spotting the heavily camouflaged enemy. Man-to-man combat at close quarters ensues.

The U.S. loses thousands of men for the sake of trivial gains: 10,000 to capture La Haye-du-Puits, 7,000 before taking the village of Sainteny. And the advance toward Saint-Lô is equally costly: one man lost for every yard gained. As one Allied general complains, "This damn war could last twenty years."

In the hell of the hedgerows, the GIs' morale wanes. The field hospitals are filled not only with wounded soldiers but those who fall prey to depression and anxiety.

July 18: The Capture of Saint-Lô

Saint-Lô is an important U.S. goal in the "war of the hedgerows" and will remain the symbol of the terrible sacrifices made by the GIs before they finally take the village on July 18.

For weeks, General Bradley's men launch one attack after another against the Panzer divisions "Das Reich" and "Lehr" and the no less formidable *Fallschirmjäger*, elite parachute commandos led by Lieutenant-General Richard Schimpf, all perched on the hills overlooking the town.

Although the Germans are forced to evacuate Saint-Lô itself on July 18, they are able to take up equally solid positions on the town's southern edge.

German infantry in camouflage attempt to make progress through the obstacles posed by the hedgerows of the Norman *bocage* countryside.
© NARA

A wounded American soldier is treated in the field.
© NARA

An American jeep enters the ruins of Saint-Lô.
© Getty Images

THE "CAPITAL OF THE RUINS"

Utterly demolished by repeated bombing throughout the month of June and by the battles that rage around it, the village of Saint-Lô earns the unenviable title of the "capital of the ruins."

The United Press war correspondent Richard McMillan is especially struck by what he finds here: "Saint-Lô reminds you of the Valley of the Shadow of Death. I don't think a single house was left standing. We had flattened it with bombs, shells, and machine-gun bullets until it was reduced to what it now was: the horrible specter of what had once been a town inhabited by human beings."

Saint-Lô after Allied bombing.
© Shorpy

American troops at the island fortress-monastery of Mont Saint-Michel off the Norman coast, July 31, 1944. © NARA

ABOVE, UPPER: **In late July 1944, General Patton** takes command of the U.S. 3rd Army, already engaged in battle, and leads the breakout from the Norman hedgerows, attacking simultaneously west into Brittany, south toward the Loire River, east toward the Seine, and north. © NARA

ABOVE, LOWER: **Allied troops enter the village of Marigny** on July 26. © NARA

SERGEANT CULIN'S HEDGE CUTTERS

An American soldier, Sergeant Curtis Culin, devises a hedge-cutter device to enable Sherman tanks to cut the hedges at the roots and pass through them safely. Culin's four-pronged plow is soldered together out of sharpened pieces of angled steel cut from the *chevaux de frise* barriers Rommel had deployed on the beaches. About 60 percent of U.S. 1st Army tanks are rapidly equipped with Culin's cutter, but the innovation is kept secret until the launch of Operation Cobra.

Breakthrough and Victory

ALLIED BREAKTHROUGHS

Piercing the German Lines: Operation Cobra

The war of the hedgerows has sorely tested the GIs, but it has not spared the enemy—as General Bradley well knows. Well informed with intelligence, much of it supplied by the Resistance, he knows that the Germans are exhausted and that their defensive formations no longer have much depth. From now on, the Allies will only have to pierce the front line to achieve permanent breakthroughs.

Such breakthroughs are the goal of Operation Cobra, which begins on July with massive aerial bombardment to the west of Saint-Lô. In the gap opened by the bombing, Bradley's divisions attack. Despite encountering initial difficulties, the Americans overwhelm the enemy within days, flattening them as they retreat in disarray, unable to reform their defenses.

The war of position yields to a war of movement. Like charging cavalry, the U.S. armored divisions sweep southward, encountering no serious opposition.

Breaking Out of the Hedgerows: Operation Bluecoat

On July 30, the British 2nd Army under General Miles Dempsey launches Operation Bluecoat, supporting the American left flank.

The offensive, originating in Caumont-L'Événté with the objective of securing the key road junction at Vire, must cross rugged *bocage* terrain which, in addition to hedgerows, is riven by steep gullies and tortuous, narrow roads, with thick vegetation and extensive minefields, all of which slow the Allied tanks. The Germans, reinforced by two divisions sent to counterattack from the Odon River sector, hold their ground in bitter fighting and retreat in an orderly fashion. Nonetheless, the British press on, and liberate Condé-sur-Noireau and Flers on August 17.

Avranches

In late July, the German army collapses and beats a hasty retreat, leaving behind nearly 20,000 prisoners. Only one week after launching their offensive, the Allies have gained 37 miles. On July 30, the Americans enter Avranches; the next day they take the bridge at Pontaubault, which has miraculously survived the war intact.

General Patton now joins the campaign at the head of the U.S. 3rd Army and immediately increases the speed of the Allied advance even more. In three days, 120,000 and 10,000 vehicles cross the Sélune River and fan out toward Brittany and the Loire Valley.

Hitler's Last Gamble

On August 7, Hitler throws the dice one last time in Normandy, launching a massive counterattack, advancing from Mortain toward Avranches in an attempt to cut the American forces in two and isolate Patton's 3rd Army.

Operation Lüttich begins at dawn, with the German tank columns making rapid progress, concealed by heavy fog. But by afternoon the sky has cleared, and swarms of Allied hunter bombers descend, pinning the Germans down and inflicting heavy losses.

In the end, Hitler's abortive attempt to turn the tables will only hasten the German defeat in Normandy.

ENCIRCLEMENT

With the failure of his counterattack in Operation Lüttich, Hitler, still vainly seeking some way to continue, delays in giving the order to withdraw. His forces are dangerously overextended westward, with their left flank exposed.

The situation gives General Bradley the idea of encircling the Germans at Mortain with a pincer maneuver by advancing the British, Canadian, and Polish forces south toward Falaise while the Americans head north toward Alençon and Argentan.

Bradley's orders to General Courtney Hodges (leading the 1st Army's 7th Corps) and General Patton (leading the 3rd Army's 15th Corps) are unambiguous: Give it all you've got, go for it!

General Leclerc and the 2nd French Armored Liberate Alençon

The 2nd French Armored Division under General Jacques-Philippe Leclerc is the only large unit of French forces to fight in the Battle of Normandy. Landing on Utah Beach in early August 1944, they are attached to Patton's U.S. 3rd Army, advancing initially toward Le Mans.

On August 10, Leclerc receives an order to change course for Alençon, which his forward units enter two days later amid a tumultuous welcome from the townspeople. But the 2nd Armored hardly has time to waste, and immediately advances toward Écouché and Argentan, trapping the enemy in the "pocket" that the Allies form south of Falaise.

Canadian and Polish Forces en Route to Falaise

Despite their success in capturing Caen, the Canadians are blocked by Panzer divisions a few miles south of the city. However, in late July and early August the Germans are forced to move a major portion of their tanks toward the western

ABOVE, UPPER: **Destroyed armor abandoned by a unit of the Panzer Division "Das Reich,"** not far from the train station of the village of Mortain.
© NARA

ABOVE, LOWER: **A forward medical post near Mortain.** After a German surprise attack, the U.S. Army 30th Infantry Division is forced to evacuate the village, with severe losses.

LEFT: **The 2nd French Armored Division,** led by General Philippe, Comte de Hauteclocque (better known by his Resistance name, Jacques-Philippe Leclerc), lands on French soil on August 1, 1944, near Saint-Martin-de-Varreville. Leclerc was captured by German forces in Champagne in 1940, but escaped, crossing France by bicycle and, via Spain and Portugal, reaching England, where he joined de Gaulle.
Caen Memorial

"All the way to Warsaw, via Normandy and Berlin!" For Polish troops, it is time for revenge.
© Library and Archives Canada

end of the front, at first to counter the offensives of Cobra and Bluecoat, then to support the counterattack at Mortain. German defenses south of Caen are dangerously weakened and the road to Falaise looks clear.

The Canadian 1st Army, reinforced by the Polish 1st Armored Division General Stanisław Maczek, is tasked with breaking through what remains of the German defenses in operations code-named Totalize and Tractable. Despite strong German resistance, the Canadians finally reach Falaise on August 17.

The Falaise Pocket

The Allies' objective is to entrap the German 7th Army and 5th Panzer Army. In order to achieve this, Montgomery's and Bradley's forces will have to link up south of Falaise, at Argentan. But an unfortunate series of military blunders delays the closing of the "pocket," which finally takes place ten miles to the east, between the villages of Trun and Chambois, around August 20.

Of the 100,000–150,000 Reich troops threatened with encirclement at the beginning of Bradley's operation, one-third to one-half succeed in escaping from the pocket before its closure—enough to force a heroic Polish defense on the heights of Mont Ormel, where the Poles hold out despite being surrounded by the

Germans for three days, sustaining (and inflicting) heavy losses, and culminating with a Polish victory at point-blank range as their ammunition runs out. The Allies take about 40,000 to 50,000 prisoners; estimates of German casualties range up to 15,000 killed. Nonetheless, contrary to popular legend, the Falaise Pocket was no "Stalingrad in Normandy."

The Corridor of Death

Bombed relentlessly by aviation and artillery, the Falaise pocket is progressively shrunk under pressure from the Allied armies until only a narrow passage a few miles wide is left between Trun and Chambois, blocked in the east by Mont Ormel, where the Poles are charged with preventing the fleeing Germans' escape. This "Corridor of Death" becomes a veritable hell heaped with the corpses of men and horses tangled in the wrecks of abandoned vehicles and incinerated artillery. Visiting the Chambois pocket, General Eisenhower remarks: "The battlefield at Falaise was unquestionably one of the greatest 'killing fields' of any of the war areas. Forty-eight hours after the closing of the gap, I was conducted through it on foot, to encounter scenes that could be described only by Dante. It was literally possible to walk for hundreds of yards at a time, stepping on nothing but dead and decaying flesh."

The **"Corridor of Death"** strewn with mangled German tanks and artillery amid ruins in the battle's aftermath.
© Imperial War Museum

GERMAN RETREAT TOWARD THE SEINE

Although the German forces in Normandy have not been destroyed in the Falaise Pocket, they are nonetheless in no condition to contain their adversary. By late August, the Germans are in full retreat toward the Seine and, beyond the river, toward the shrinking borders of the Reich.

The Allies work hard to encircle the enemy in a new pocket south of the river but fail to advance quickly enough. All the bridges over the Seine downstream from Paris have been destroyed. However, with various improvised methods, the Germans succeed in getting 200,000 men across the river, at the cost of abandoning most of their heavy artillery. The German withdrawal proceeds in orderly fashion despite continued attacks from Allied aviation, which is somewhat hindered by overcast skies.

The Germans continue to withdraw, pursued by the British, Canadian, and Polish forces across Upper Normandy and on into Belgium. The western part of the *département* of Calvados as well as Eure are quickly liberated. Montgomery's armies reach the Seine at the end of August, crossing on floating bridges at Vernon and Elbeuf, and continue their rapid advance. However, they leave behind the fortress of Le Havre, where the German garrison is well dug in. After a lethal aerial bombardment and a brief siege, the city falls on September 12.

In the ruins of the town of Lisieux a Feldgendarm (military policeman) gives directions to a retreating German convoy headed for the Seine.
© Bundesarchiv

The German retreat: men, horses, and vehicles prepare to cross the Seine in late August 1944.
© ECPAD

German prisoners of war in an Allied prison camp near d'Alençon.
Caen Memorial

In liberated Cherbourg.
© NARA

VICTORY

Victory in Normandy Hastens the Liberation of France

After being devastated in Normandy, the German army is no longer capable of opposing the Allies' rapid advance. Patton reaches Verdun on August 31; Montgomery is in Brussels by September 3.

While the enemy is already retreating through Normandy, Free French and American forces land in southern France, in Provence, on August 15. After taking Toulon and Marseille, with the support of units of the Free Forces of the Interior (FFI), resistance fighters organized into light infantry units in liberated territory, the Allies clean out the Rhône corridor and enter Lyon on September 3. To avoid being caught in a trap, the German forces evacuate the southwest, under pressure from the FFI.

The linkup between the Allied armies advancing from Normandy and Provence takes place on September 12, between Troyes and Dijon.

By early autumn, most of French territory has been liberated, except for Alsace in the northeast, on the German border, and the "Atlantic pockets," harbor towns such as La Rochelle, which have been bypassed by the main thrust of the Allied invasion, most of which will remain in German hands until Germany's general surrender in May 1945.

Assessing the Costs

General Eisenhower will write in his memoirs, there is a great difference between a battle plan and its outcome.

The Battle of Normandy has lasted for twelve weeks instead of three, owing to German resistance pushed to extremes—indeed, to the point of collapse. However, from this point forward, every Allied plan is turned upside down, but now with positive results. Most of France is liberated much faster than the strategists of Operation Overlord could ever have imagined: "The campaign of 1940 in reverse," as General Leclerc will say.

Long and painful, the battles in Normandy have cost the lives of 37,000 Allied soldiers and 55,000 Germans, not to mention the 20,000 civilian victims of the confrontation.

Allied bombing drives Normans onto the roads.
Caen Memorial

Civilians in Battle

Over the course of summer 1944, the people of Normandy find themselves brutally plunged into the heart of one of the most massive confrontations of World War II.

During the heaviest combat, in July, 2 million soldiers clash in the *départements* of La Manche and Calvados, whose total civilian population is less than 1 million.

Some find themselves within the bridgehead established by the Allies, which diminishes the risks they face without, however, eliminating them. Others, less fortunate, are trapped along the line of fire or within the zones still in German hands. For them, there is nothing to do, for better or worse, but to seek shelter from the bombs, shells, and bullets.

Aerial Bombing

Of all the painful memories that scar the Normans who live through the battles of summer 1944, the most terrifying are unquestionably those of the dreadful bombing unleashed by Allied aviation—which Nazi and Vichy propaganda does not neglect to exploit in spring 1944, with the release of a torrent of posters, news-

paper articles, and radio broadcasts against the "liberator."

The Vichy government even proposes to crisscross the country with a traveling exhibition carried on the back of a truck to show the French people the ravages of Allied bombing. Marshal Pétain himself visits the devastated cities and towns. Starting in Paris in April, he travels next to Rouen on May 14, timing his visit to coincide with the second Sunday in May, France's official national commemoration of the Maid of Orleans and Rouen's annual Joan of Arc Festival. The day before D-Day, the collaborationist press publishes numerous reports from Normandy, attempting to exploit civilian suffering to rouse French public opinion against Allied forces.

The aerial bombing alone is responsible for 60 percent of the civilian death toll during the Battle of Normandy.

Normans Take to the Roads

Throughout the summer of 1944, nearly 150,000 Normans are forced to quit their homes, taking their chances on the roads in a mass exodus fraught with danger. The first to leave are refugees from the Allied urban bombing of June 6–7. Next it is the turn of villagers driven out

In the ruins of Caen.
© Imperial War Museum

Surviving Underground
During the long siege of Caen, in order to hide from the bombs, thousands of the Caennais and villagers from the neighboring rural *communes* seek shelter underground in cellars and tunnels, and above all in the ancient limestone quarries that surround the city, where the famous *pierre de Caen*, or Caen stone, was formerly dug.
© Imperial War Museum

Temporary German graves near Carentan.
© Imperial War Museum

Refugees of the Abbaye aux Hommes
Although the entire city center of Caen, devastated by the bombing of June 6–7, is nothing more than a desert of ruins, several thousand Caennais find shelter in the buildings of the Abbaye aux Hommes, a former abbey church that had at the time been converted into a secondary school, and in the abbey church of Saint-Étienne.
© Library and Archives Canada

by the approaching battlefront, most often ordered to leave by German troops. The evacuation reaches its peak in July, affecting mainly the people of La Manche and the countryside south of Caen.

Many refugees go no farther than the neighboring *département*; others will press on much farther, heading for the Loire Valley or central France. Their return will be slow and for some will take many months.

Prisoners Shot in Caen
During the Battle of Normandy, nearly five hundred people from the region are executed by the Nazis for their involvement in Resistance actions, for coming to the aid of Allied soldiers, or simply for refusing to obey the Germans' orders or to fulfill their requisitions.

The most tragic instance is the German massacre of inmates in the prison in Caen, where about a hundred members of the Resistance arrested in the months preceding D-Day are held, awaiting deportation to concentration camps in Germany.

On the morning of June 6, having failed to secure any means of evacuating the prisoners eastward in France, the head of the Gestapo in Caen decides to summarily execute 75 to 80 of the inmates on the spot.

Normandy Pays the Price for the Liberation of France
Normany is liberated, but at terrible human and material cost: its cities and towns are razed, its villages laid waste, its historic monuments vanished forever, its economy in ruins—and 20,000 civilians killed.

Such is the result of a battle that lasted much longer than anticipated, inflicting on the Normans a heavy burden of mourning amid heaps of ruins. The rest of France mainly escapes the Norman catastrophe, being rapidly liberated in the wake of the general retreat of the shattered German armies.

In this sense, it is fair to say that Normandy paid the price for the liberation of France.

Celebrating the Liberation
The Liberation in Normandy leaves those who live through it with two contrasting images: the destruction and death caused by the ferocious battles and the joy of freedom recovered after four long years of occupation. The people of Normandy erupt in rejoicing, exulting all the

more in areas where the people have not directly suffered the horrors of war. Flags and banners fly from every window; the Allied colors are even displayed on clothes quickly stitched together to welcome the liberators.

French children are especially drawn to the debonair soldiers who freely share their chocolate, candy, and chewing gum.

July 14, 1944

Forbidden by the Germans and the Vichy government, patriotic displays and demonstrations have disappeared during the Occupation, including the annual festivities on November 11 (commemorating the Allied victory in World War I) and July 14 (Bastille Day, the French national holiday). It is no surprise then that the French fête July 14, 1944, with unparalleled fervor in every liberated town and village across the country, as Allied troops join the local people to celebrate in style. ■

Preparing to celebrate the Liberation in Carentan. © NARA

Liberated French youngsters cheer for passing U.S. soldiers. © NARA

Bibliography

Alary, Éric. *Les Français au quotidian, 1939–1949*. Paris: Perrin, 2006.

Audoin-Rouzeau, Stéphane et al., eds. *La violence de guerre 1914–1945: approches comparées des deux conflits mondiaux*. Paris: Éditions Complexe, in the series Histoire du Temps Présent, 2002.

Azéma, Jean-Pierre and François Bédarida, eds. *La France des années noires*, vol. 2, *De l'occupation à la Libération*. Paris: Seuil, 1993.

Beevor, Antony. *Stalingrad: The Fateful Siege, 1942–1943*. London: Penguin, 1998.

Bovy, Daniel. *Dictionnaire de la barbarie nazie et de la Shoah*. Brussels: Éditions Luc Pire, in the series Voix de la Mémoire / Liège: Les Territoires de la Mémoire, 2007 (co-publication).

Brayard, Florent, ed. *Le génocide des Juifs: entre procès et histoire (1943–2000)*. Paris: Complexe, in the series Histoire du Temps Présent, 2000.

Browning, Christopher. *Ordinary Men: Reserve Police Battalion 101 and the Final Solution in Poland*. New York: HarperCollins, 1992.

Burrin, Philippe. *La France à l'heure allemande: 1940–1944*. Paris: Seuil, 1995.

Corcy, Stéphanie. *La vie culturelle sous l'Occupation*. Paris: Perrin, 2005.

Desbois, Patrick. *The Holocaust by Bullets: A Priest's Journey to Uncover the Truth Behind the Murder of 1.5 Million Jews*. New York: Macmillan, 2009.

Eismann, Gaël, and Stefan Martens. *Occupation et répression militaire allemandes: la politique de "maintien de l'ordre" en Europe occupée, 1939–1945*. Paris: Autrement, in the series Mémoires/Histoire, 2007.

Friedländer, Saul. *The Years of Extermination: Nazi Germany and the Jews, 1939–1945*. New York: HarperCollins, 2007.

Hilberg, Raul. *The Destruction of the European Jews*, 3rd ed. New Haven, CT: Yale University Press, 2003.

Ingrao, Christian. *Les chasseurs noirs: la brigade Dirlewanger*. Paris: Perrin, 2006.

Jackson, Julian. *France: The Dark Years, 1940–1944*. New York: Oxford University Press, 2003.

Laborie, Pierre. *L'opinion française sous Vichy*. Paris: Le Seuil, in the series L'Univers Historique, 1990.

Marcot, François, ed. *Dictionnaire historique de la Résistance: résistance intérieure et France libre*. Paris: Robert Laffont, in the series Bouquins, 2006.

Margolin, Jean-Louis. *L'armée de l'empereur: violences et crimes du Japon en guerre, 1937–1945*. Paris: Armand Colin, in the series Les Enjeux de l'Histoire, 2007.

Missika, Dominique and Dominique Veillon. *Résistance: histoires de familles, 1940–1945*. Paris: Armand Colin/France Bleu, 2009.

Peschanski, Denis. *Les Tsiganes en France: 1939–1946*. Paris: CNRS, in the series Histoire du XXe Siècle, 1984.

Prazan, Mickaël. *Le massacre de Nankin, 1937: entre mémoire, oubli et negation*. Paris: Denoël, 2007.

Quellien, Jean. *Les victimes civiles du Calvados dans la bataille de Normandie: 1er mars 1944–31 décembre 1945*. Caen: Éditions du Lys, 1995.

Rousso, Henry. *Les années noires, vivre sous l'Occupation*. Paris: Gallimard, in the series Découvertes, 1992.

Semelin, Jacques. *Sans armes face à Hitler: la résistance civile en Europe, 1939–1943*. Paris: Payot, 1989.

Simonnet, Stéphane. *Atlas de la Libération de la France, 6 juin 1944–8 mai 1945: des débarquements aux villes libérées*. Paris: Autrement, in the series Atlas/Mémoires, 2004.

Virgili, Fabrice. *La France ¨virile¨: des femmes tondues à la Libération*. Paris: Payot, 2000.

Wette, Wolfram. *Les crimes de la Wehrmacht*. Paris: Perrin, 2009.

Wieviorka, Olivier. *Histoire du débarquement en Normandie: des origines à la Libération de Paris, 1941–1944*. Paris: Le Seuil, 2007.

Translator's Note

Guerre mondiale—Guerre totale (World War—Total War), the French text of which the present volume is a translation, documents the largest-scale renovation and expansion of the Caen Memorial since its inauguration in 1988.

There is probably no way for a translator to make the English-speaking reader aware of every nuance involved. Where it seems to me necessary, I have sought to make the implicit explicit, to raise subtext to the level of text, to gloss and expand upon key names and terms to the extent that space allows. For example, the mere mention of such figures as Pétain and Moulin evokes in any French reader a vast shared knowledge, while many American readers may not even recognize the names. On a purely mechanical level, I have also added translations or summaries of French text within illustrations (slogans and signs and suchlike). Throughout, I hope that I have preserved the writers' distinctive tones of voice and hewn close to their intentions.

By coincidence, I am fortunate to have visited the Caen Memorial several years ago; I felt that I could not travel through Normandy on my way to Juno Beach without seeing the museum (being Canadian by birth, I was particularly preoccupied with the role of Canadian forces in the liberation of France). While the Memorial is designed primarily to inform, to enlighten, I found my visit one of the most moving experiences I have ever had in a museum. I can only echo the authors of this book's preface: if you can, reader, let this book spur you to go to Caen and see for yourself.

CHRISTOPHER CAINES